Praise for *Risk Parity*

"A must-read for anyone investing in the market who wants to maximize upside return while minimizing downside risk. Alex has skillfully crafted a 'how to' book that spells out, step-by-step, building a balanced portfolio that can generate equity-like returns across a diverse spectrum of asset classes without the concomitant risk of equity securities, a strategy that will deliver in the long run no matter the market or economic environment. His proven, no-nonsense approach is communicated in such a refreshingly straightforward manner that it can be easily understood and applied in practice by novice investors while simultaneously educating and informing the savviest wealth manager. If you're laboring under the belief that a balanced portfolio is 60% stocks and 40% bonds, then this book is for you. *Risk Parity* will change your life—and your wallet!"

—**Lloyd Greif,** President and CEO, Greif & Co.; Founder, Lloyd Greif Center for Entrepreneurial Studies at the University of Southern California's Marshall School of Business

"Alex has written a book that perfectly encapsulates why his vision and perspective on finances is so deeply respected. I've been lucky enough to have his wisdom and guidance around risk parity investing and now you can, too."

—**Greg Berlanti,** writer, producer, and director

"This book is an excellent roadmap for understanding both how, and more importantly why, risk parity strategies work. Alex deftly explains the differences between a 60/40 portfolio and a more balanced strategy."

—**Bill Lee,** former CIO, Kaiser Permanente

"When done right, diversification can be the key to producing better investment returns over the long haul—yet not enough investors have been paying enough attention. For this reason, I consider *Risk Parity* one of the best portfolio strategy books for growth investors and money managers."

—**Daniel Martins,** Founder, DM Martins Capital Management; regular contributor to Seeking Alpha

"Alex shows that the standard portfolio of stocks and bonds may be a lot riskier than most people realize. This is a terrific critique of conventional thinking on asset allocation."

—**Brett Arends,** MarketWatch columnist

Risk Parity

How to Invest for All Market Environments

Alex Shahidi

WILEY

Published by John Wiley & Sons, Inc., Hoboken, New Jersey.
Published simultaneously in Canada.

For general information on our other products and services or for technical support,
please contact our Customer Care Department within the United States at (800)
762-2974, outside the United States at (317) 572-3993, or fax (317) 572-4002.

Wiley publishes in a variety of print and electronic formats and by print-on-demand.
Some material included with standard print versions of this book may not be included
in e-books or in print-on-demand. If this book refers to media such as a CD or DVD that
is not included in the version you purchased, you may download this material at http://
booksupport.wiley.com. For more information about Wiley products, visit www.wiley.com.

Library of Congress Cataloging-in-Publication Data

Names: Shahidi, Alex, author.
Title: Risk parity : how to invest for all market environments / Alex   Shahidi.
Description: Hoboken, New Jersey : John Wiley & Sons, Inc., [2022] | Includes index.
Identifiers: LCCN 2021031557 (print) | LCCN 2021031558 (ebook) | ISBN
    9781119812562 (hardback) | ISBN 9781119812432 (adobe pdf) | ISBN
    9781119812425 (epub)
Subjects: LCSH: Risk management. | Portfolio management.
Classification: LCC HD61 .S389 2022 (print) | LCC HD61 (ebook) | DDC
    658.15/5—dc23

LC record available at https://lccn.loc.gov/2021031557
LC ebook record available at https://lccn.loc.gov/2021031558

Cover Design: Wiley
Cover Image: © Dimitri Otis/Getty Images
SKY10030226_111121

I dedicate this book to the investors with curiosity to learn and open-mindedness to overcome convention.

Contents

Foreword

Alex is doing a great service to the savers and investors of the world and, in particular, those who are responsible for their livelihood in retirement. Statistics show that the average individual investor has substantially under-performed most passively held asset mixes. And the history of markets shows that every asset class in every country over the past 200 years has suffered massive wealth destruction at one time or another, meaning a decline in real purchasing power of 50% to 80% within the course of a decade. Even cash is a very risky asset when you view it through the lens of inflation-adjusted returns. Today, cash and bonds are particularly risky, because policy makers have pushed real interest rates into negative territory and are holding them there as a means of reducing the burdens on debtors, shifting that burden to the retirements of savers and asset holders.

In recognition of the risks, we at Bridgewater believe that the most reliable solution is a balanced portfolio. By balanced I mean a portfolio whose risk allocation is distributed across a set of asset classes which have offsetting exposures to shifts in the economic environment. Shifts in economic growth and inflation exert a dominant influence on asset returns. Therefore, you want a mix of assets that neutralizes these influences on returns.

At Bridgewater we refer to this as the All Weather approach: a portfolio that is balanced to the influences of economic growth and inflation, enabling performance across all environments. Many of us have applied this All Weather approach for decades to our own personal portfolios and for the largest and most sophisticated institutional investors in the world. In time, the approach has become known as Risk Parity, and a number of professional asset managers developed their own way of doing it. There are significant differences, but what they all have in common is a balanced allocation of risk across complementary asset classes.

What Alex is doing in this book is making this balanced approach available to anyone who wants reliability of investment returns over time, regardless of how economic conditions transpire. There is no fluff or bluster in the book. Each chapter is a relevant building block toward a well-balanced whole. This is not a book of empty assertions or unproven theories. It is backed up by research and logic, which he presents in each chapter. The research and logic have been borne out through time.

We at Bridgewater have known Alex for a very long time and can attest to the thoughtfulness and thoroughness of his approach. He describes his journey; we watched it unfold first-hand. There is legitimacy and authenticity to what follows. I hope that you take it seriously and put it into action.

Bob Prince
Co-CIO, Bridgewater Associates

Preface

A fundamental question all investors face is whether they want their portfolio to be balanced or imbalanced. Framing the decision in this simple way leads to an obvious answer. Why would anyone not desire good balance, particularly when a portfolio can be easily diversified without sacrificing long-term returns?

Surprisingly, nearly every portfolio that I have observed over the past couple of decades has been poorly balanced. These portfolios are overly sensitive to shifting economic environments, performing brilliantly during good times and underperforming the rest of the time. In fact, it seems that investors have become accustomed to their portfolios rising and falling along with the stock market's wild swings. We cheer on bull markets and suffer through the inevitable downturns as we are all in the market together. Investors have been conditioned to believe that attractive long-term returns can only be attained by allocating a large percentage of their portfolio to stocks, which can be highly volatile. Those who can't stomach the ride should not participate.

I wrote this book with the aim of debunking this widely held myth. I introduce an easy-to-follow conceptual framework that allows for strong balance while targeting long-term returns competitive with equities. This is not an approach that involves market timing, a sophisticated trading strategy, or the use of esoteric investment vehicles. A simple, fixed allocation across a diversified mix of major asset classes is all that is needed to achieve the objective.

The investment strategy, commonly termed "Risk Parity," is not something new and untested. Some of the world's most sophisticated institutions have adopted and successfully implemented this approach for several decades. Bridgewater Associates, the largest hedge fund in the world, developed the concepts presented in this book over 25 years ago and has been running a risk parity strategy for its giant institutional portfolios ever since.

It seems that investors' portfolios are not only imbalanced, but that investors don't have a full understanding of what it means to be balanced. I want to share these insights that I have gleaned from the smartest minds in the industry because every investor, large and small, deserves to know. In this book, I attempt to describe the framework in a language that anyone interested in investing will understand regardless of their investment acumen and experience. Over the years, I have had the opportunity to walk through the concepts with a wide variety of investors and investment professionals. With repetition comes an appreciation of the points that resonate and a refined narrative for more complex topics.

Moreover, I feel strongly that investors need more balance today than perhaps at any point in our lifetimes. The potential range of economic outcomes is exceedingly broad, and the odds of extreme results only seem to increase over time. My goal is to equip investors with the knowledge and tools they need to build smarter portfolios and avoid taking unnecessary risk.

Acknowledgments

The author is not the sole writer of a book. The ideas presented were likely sparked by someone else. The manner in which the concepts are described was probably polished from constructive feedback from the audience. One of the greatest challenges writers face is appropriately zooming out to ensure the overall message is clear when we are deeply immersed in the current paragraph that we strive to perfect. Thoughtful feedback from friends, family, and colleagues who offered a fresh perspective of the big picture enabled me to stay on course.

Damien Bisserier, my business partner since 2014 and close friend long before then, has not only taught me the intricate details of the risk parity approach but also how to tell the story. Damien worked at Bridgewater Associates for nearly a decade, so he was steeped in these concepts and was trained by the most sophisticated proponents of the strategy to effectively convey the concepts. I have immensely benefited from his hard work and brilliance for many years and would like to acknowledge his contribution.

Michael Marco, a valued colleague of mine at Evoke Advisors and former Investment Associate at Bridgewater, provided extremely insightful feedback throughout this process. His unique background and time commitment to carefully read the entire manuscript was an invaluable asset in this journey. Thank you Michael.

My deepest gratitude goes to the entire Bridgewater organization, particularly to Jim Haskel, Ray Dalio, Bob Prince, and Greg Jensen, all of whom were integral in familiarizing me with the concepts presented in this book many years ago. Without my connection to Bridgewater and their support to write this book (and my previous book), none of this would have made it to print.

Brendan Corcoran and Aman Ahluwalia, who work with me at Evoke, took the time to read every word and offer valuable comments. I recognize that they both had little time to spare, so I appreciate their commitment to help. I am also thankful for the contributions of the following partners at Evoke: David Hou, Mark Sear, Kim Ip, Darell Krasnoff, Andrew Palmer, and Eric Bright. I appreciate your interest on the subject and input into the process.

Eric Schwartz, Abigail Johnson, Mike Miller, Diane Mirowski, Corey Barash, Aaron Iba, and Andrew Gwozdz dove in and thoughtfully shared their views. Each comes from a very different background, which provides a unique perspective that helped shape how the book was written.

The team at Wiley deserves recognition for the countless hours spent on this project. It all started with Bill Falloon, who gave me an opportunity to publish my first book seven years ago. Thank you for taking a chance on an inexperienced author and for trusting me to write a second one. Purvi Patel and Samantha Enders, your professionalism and dedication to develop my manuscript into the final product is greatly appreciated. It has been an absolute joy working with all of you.

Finally, I am thankful for my soulmate of over 20 years, Danielle, and our precious children, Michael and Bella, for their continued support throughout. Their persistent encouragement fueled me through writing challenges I faced along the way and helped me stay focused on the finish line.

About the Author

Alex Shahidi is a Managing Partner and Co-Chief Investment Officer at Evoke Advisors, a $21 billion registered investment advisor. Alex has more than 20 years of experience as an investment consultant managing billions of dollars for institutional and ultra-high-net-worth clients. He began his career at Merrill Lynch, where he led one of the firm's largest institutional consulting groups, advising more than $10 billion in assets with an average client size of approximately $300 million. After Merrill, Alex co-founded Advanced Research Investment Solutions (ARIS), where he, along with co-founder Damien Bisserier, oversaw the firm's research and client service efforts.

Alex is a Chartered Financial Analyst (CFA®), a Certified Investment Management Analyst (CIMA®), a Certified Financial Planner (CFP®), and a Chartered Financial Consultant (ChFC®). *Barron's* magazine has repeatedly ranked him as one of America's Top 100 Independent Financial Advisors, Top 1,200 Financial Advisors, and Top 1,000 Financial Advisors.

Alex graduated cum laude from the University of California, Santa Barbara, with degrees in business economics and law. He earned a JD from the University of California, Hastings Law School, and is a member of the bar in California.

Alex's first book, *Balanced Asset Allocation: How to Profit in Any Economic Climate*, was published by Wiley in 2014. The article introducing the premise of the book was recognized with the IMCA 2012 Stephen L. Kessler Writing Award as well as in the *Wall Street Journal, Market Watch, Money News*, Fidelity.com, and *Wall Street Daily*.

Alex has been interviewed on Bloomberg Television and Radio, BBC World News, and Yahoo Finance and for articles in the *Wall Street Journal, Barron's*, and other major publications. He has also been featured in numerous podcasts including *Capital Allocators, The Investor's Podcast*, and *Seeking Alpha*.

Introduction

My business partners and I have been on a multidecade journey to discover the optimal portfolio. We recognize that we will never reach the destination of this lifelong crusade – investing is like an impossible puzzle that has no perfect solution. But we have set out as our mission to endlessly progress toward the ultimate goal. Fortunately, we have the opportunity to explore potential answers with some of the most sophisticated investors in the world. As Co-Chief Investment Officer of Evoke Advisors, a multibillion-dollar SEC-registered investment advisor in Los Angeles, I regularly engage with well-respected investment managers and industry thought leaders. We at Evoke have also been blessed to build a network of some of the greatest investment minds of our time, including CIOs of leading institutional investors and founders of the world's largest and most successful money managers. As students of the market with an intense focus, we have gleaned insight over the years from repeated interactions with the smartest investors who are also searching for similar investment answers.

Investing can be incredibly humbling. Mistakes are inevitable and seem to conveniently transpire just when you think you've figured it all out. This is evidently one of those industries in which the more you learn the more you realize how little you know. It is interesting to take a step back and observe that we know so much more now than we did 20 years ago, but that only means that we will certainly be more knowledgeable 20 years from now. This simple recognition is imperative because it prevents complacency and forces us to march on and continue the search. The crystallization of the end goal also makes it easier to find other like-minded individuals from whom we can expand our learning.

For me, a monumental step forward occurred in 2005 when I was first introduced to Bridgewater Associates. As an institutional investment consultant at Merrill Lynch, I was seeking insightful investment managers to allocate the billions of dollars that were entrusted to my team and me. Our group was founded and led by John Ebey, one of the brightest investment minds I have met to this day. John is also one of the most genuine, charming, and generous individuals I have ever known. However, his greatest talent may be his remarkable storytelling abilities. He's the one who originally discovered Bridgewater, which he eloquently conveys in a story that I repeat next.

Bridgewater is the largest hedge fund in the world and typically only works with major pools of capital such as sovereign wealth funds, enormous pension plans, and college endowments. Unlike most investment firms, they typically do not cater to high-net-worth individuals, evidenced by their current stated minimum client size of $5 billion! John had known of Bridgewater by reading about them and hearing good things from investors he highly respected. John is not bashful, particularly when it comes to pursuing solutions to investment problems for clients. He called Bridgewater's front desk and asked to speak with an investment professional who would answer his questions about their strategies. No one returned his call. He tried again and again without success. He concluded that the likely reason for the lack of response was that he worked at Merrill Lynch, which is better known for advising wealthy families (rather than institutions with over $5 billion in assets).

John's persistence eventually paid off and he was able to set up a time to meet with someone at the firm. He flew from Los Angeles to Bridgewater's campus in rural Westport, Connecticut. Thanks to his charming demeanor, the meeting swiftly transitioned from the normal discussion about investment philosophy to him instantly gaining favor. He was introduced to the top professionals in the firm shortly thereafter and eventually became one of Bridgewater's favorite clients. They even studied his presentation style and asked for tips to better inform how they interacted with clients.

The next time Bridgewater was in Los Angeles, John set up a time for me to meet them. I was captivated by their unique approach from that initial meeting, and I set out to learn as much as I could from this organization. John started to allocate our client capital to Bridgewater's strategies, officially launching my multidecade relationship with this firm.

Bridgewater is first and foremost a research organization. They have been publishing their "Daily Observations" every business day for over 30 years. These deliberately private pieces are reserved for their clients, and they are designed to provide an over-the-shoulder peak into the firm's latest thinking. The Daily Observations are widely considered so insightful that they have essentially become required reading for managers of the largest pools of capital across the globe and for leading central bankers and policymakers. My first task upon discovery of this gold mine was to download and print every Daily Observations in their client archive. My reading stack of past "wires," as they are commonly termed, measured over six inches thick and continued to grow since new wires came out every day. I read every single one and attained more investment knowledge in three months than I had collected in my previous six years.

Ray Dalio founded Bridgewater in 1975. Ray is among the most successful and highly regarded investors of all time and one of the wealthiest individuals in the world. Ray hired my business partner, Damien Bisserier, at Bridgewater in 2004, when the firm had about 200 employees (today they have over 1,500). Damien started his Bridgewater career in the research department and worked his way to a client-facing role because of his passion for helping sophisticated institutions solve complex investment problems. I was one of Damien's clients, which is how we originally connected.

The year 2007 was a major turning point. Damien set up a meeting with Ray and me, which was the first time that I had ever met him in person. He explained the origins of his investment philosophy and what led to his work that formed the foundation for his All Weather portfolio, which is commonly referred to as "risk parity" today. Ray had been searching for years for a simple portfolio that could be used to manage his family's assets for generations. As a professional investor he appreciated the difficulty of timing markets and generating "alpha," so his goal was to identify an investment solution that was completely passive: a set-it-and-forget-it portfolio that is designed to deliver attractive returns while surviving all the bumps along the way. He walked me through the logical sequence for his pioneering work and creation of All Weather.

It was a memorable hour that culminated in my asking a simple question: If this is so obvious, then why is this approach so different from the conventional portfolio? Ray said that he had grappled with that very question for years and finally concluded that it was because of a lack of smart, independent thinkers. We are educated in school to read and regurgitate what we learned on exams and papers. Those who master this process tend to excel in school and earn highly coveted job offers. At work, they are generally trained to follow the lead of others before them, and the process repeats itself. Rarely are we encouraged to challenge convention and discern the truth by investigating the core issues ourselves. Inertia and peer risk can also play material roles in prolonging the status quo. Both can prevent adoption of new approaches even when there's agreement that it is better. The pull to follow others and the risk of being different and looking wrong can be powerful forces that require both independent thinking as well as high conviction to overcome.

To reach the All Weather framework he had to challenge the assumptions he had been taught at Harvard Business School and through broadly accepted investment tenets. He had to think independently to, in effect, reinvent the proverbial wheel. One of Ray's gifts is his intuitive drive to avoid blindly accepting traditional perspectives and to start from the most basic level to uncover his own conclusions. He described it as going from assumption A to assumption B and so on until you reach the conclusion. Most people don't go back to A, they start at E since it is widely viewed as the truth. If you start at E, then you end up in the same place as everyone else, but if you start at A you end up where he did.

I learned from Ray not to accept investment assumptions on their face without doing the independent work to determine if I arrive at the same point. Therefore, I took what he taught me and set out to figure it out on my own. This sparked a multiyear research project and development of a 10,000-page Excel spreadsheet as I studied 100 years of financial market data. Of course, I ended up in the exact same place as Ray and eventually published my findings in my first book, *Balanced Asset Allocation: How to Profit in Any Economic Climate*, which was published by Wiley in 2014. Ray and Bridgewater were strongly supportive of the project and instrumental in providing me with the required data to back my findings.

Damien called me after my first meeting with Ray to let me know that Ray enjoyed our encounter and hoped that I would join Bridgewater. I managed to flip the discussion by explaining to Damien why I loved my career and my position of helping my clients, and I would never consider a change. That led to an ongoing dialogue about possibly working together at some point in the future. Over time, we realized that we were completely aligned in our mission to strive to continually improve client portfolios and our belief about how an ideal business should be managed. Six years later Damien got married and decided it was time to move back to California to be closer to his family and to raise a family of his own. He left Bridgewater in 2013 after a successful nine-year career and took 10 months off to travel to 23 countries on an extended honeymoon. Damien joined me when I departed Merrill Lynch after 15 years, and we launched our own firm, Advanced Research Investment Solutions (ARIS), in 2014. This marked another major inflection point in my career.

ARIS managed over $12 billion in client assets for many years and was consistently ranked among the top advisory firms in the country by *Barron's*.[1] We implemented the investment framework, which was described in my first book, across our client portfolios. Five years after founding ARIS, we created the Advanced Research Risk Parity Index as a proxy for the investment approach. This allowed us to back test and publish the results over a long period of time through shifting economic environments.

This brings us to the present. The reason I wrote this book is to describe the thought process that has led our journey to risk parity. My goal is to memorialize our learning over the past 15 years in simple-to-understand, nontechnical language that anyone who is interested in investing can absorb. I begin with bigger-picture topics and work my way down to the details. For those who enjoyed my first book, this may essentially be viewed as a second, more refined edition that is tailored for the specific risk parity index that we created. I strive to present this information to you so you can objectively decide for yourself whether the framework is sound.

The book is divided into the following chapters:

❑ Chapter 1 describes the conceptual framework for risk parity. I will explain what it means to be well balanced and why the conventional portfolio is surprisingly poorly balanced.

❑ Chapter 2 gets into the two required steps to build balance: (1) selecting the right asset classes, and (2) structuring each to have similar returns.

❑ Chapters 3–7 dive into the major asset classes used in our risk parity model. I explain what they are, how they perform in different economic environments, and their role in a balanced mix of assets.

❑ Chapter 8 lays out the details of our risk parity portfolio, including the desired weighting to each asset class and, most important, the rationale for the specific allocation.

---

[1] The *Barron's* Top RIA Firms rankings are based on data provided by over 4,000 of the nation's most productive advisors. Factors used in the rankings include: assets under management, revenue produced for the firm, regulatory record, technology spending, staff diversity, succession planning, quality of practice, and philanthropic work. Investment performance isn't an explicit component because not all advisors have audited results and because performance figures often are influenced more by clients' risk tolerance than by an advisor's investment-picking abilities. Barron's is a registered trademark of Dow Jones & Company, L.P. All rights reserved.

The Risk Parity Portfolio
- 25% global equities
- 25% commodities (15% commodity producer equities, 10% gold)
- 35% long-term Treasuries
- 35% long-term TIPS

❑ Chapter 9 provides a long-term historical return series to show how the risk parity portfolio would have performed through varying market environments.

❑ Chapter 10 covers the timeliness of the risk parity approach. Given the wide range of potential economic outcomes looking forward, today appears to be a prudent time for investors to maintain strong balance.

❑ Chapter 11 gets into the "rebalancing boost," which refers to the increase in returns that comes from a repeated process of buying low and selling high.

❑ Chapter 12 covers implementation strategies to put the concepts into practice.

❑ Chapter 13 points out the unique environments during which the risk parity portfolio may be expected to perform poorly. I think of this chapter as a "Break in Case of Emergency" warning. It serves as a reminder to adopters of risk parity to read this section if tempted to abandon the strategy.

❑ Chapter 14 summarizes my responses to the most commonly raised questions and objections I've heard about risk parity over the past 15 years.

❑ Chapter 15 offers some concluding remarks.

CHAPTER ONE

What Is Risk Parity?

R ay Dalio, Bob Prince and their team at Bridgewater pioneered most of the concepts presented in this book about 30 years ago and have been successfully refining and implementing the strategy ever since. Our risk parity mix uses the same overall framework as Bridgewater's, although the specific asset classes and allocation represent a simplified version. Our approach also differs slightly as it is designed for a wide range of investors, many of whom are subject to paying taxes, as opposed to being tailored for the largest tax-exempt institutions in the world. This also represents our best thinking as of this writing. As previously stated, we hope to continue to evolve our understanding and make improvements in future iterations.

RISK PARITY IS ALL ABOUT BALANCE

The ultimate goal of a risk parity portfolio is to *earn attractive equity-like returns* while taking *less risk than equities*. Both objectives are important. We want good absolute returns (competitive with equities) over the long run since that is the main purpose behind investing capital. Controlling risk is also paramount because losses are painful and can be difficult to recover from, both mathematically and emotionally. A portfolio that achieves attractive returns while minimizing risk can be constructed with a *well-balanced allocation* that invests in public market securities, which will be the focus here.

The operative term is *balance*. Webster's dictionary defines *balance* as a "state in which different things have an equal or proper amount of importance." Ideally, we should seek balance in all aspects of life. From the most basic level, we hope to equally distribute our weight so we can stand upright without falling. We should probably also strive to maintain a balanced diet or appropriate work-life balance. Many of us have discovered that excessive and prolonged imbalance in these areas often ends in a painful outcome that forces us back toward better balance.

Within the context of an investment portfolio, balance has a comparable connotation and is similarly important. In a portfolio, balance means giving similar importance, or weight, to asset classes that behave differently from each other. A balanced portfolio has some assets that perform well when others perform poorly. As a result, the portfolio is not overly exposed or vulnerable to a particular market or economic outcome. Instead, no matter what happens, the portfolio is reasonably well protected. This is what it means to have a "well-diversified" portfolio. A diversified portfolio is one that minimizes risk for a given level of return. Said differently, the objective is to take risk efficiently so that we don't take unnecessary risk when a similar return can be earned through a smoother path that experiences less frequent and less severe drawdowns.

A Smoother Path

Starting from a high-level conceptual framework, a smoother path can be attained by investing across a wide range of return streams that are different from one another. By different, I mean that while they all go up over time, their ups and downs generally do not coincide. As a result, a total portfolio that is made up of these fluctuating constituents should exhibit less variability over time than any single one of them. This is the core insight of Modern Portfolio Theory, which posits that a portfolio made up of diverse components can exhibit less risk for a given level of return than a less diversified mix. The bold line in Figure 1.1 illustrates the conceptual idea of a smoother path – one that takes less risk to earn a similar return.

If we strive to grow the portfolio from Point A to Point B, allocating across multiple assets that all end at Point B but proceed through different paths yields a less bumpy ride for the total portfolio. A good metaphor for this framework is an automobile engine. The engine is made up of a diverse mix of parts: pistons, cylinders, chains, spark plugs, crankshafts, valves, and so on. Each component is necessary and functions very differently from the other parts. Each has a pre-defined role to ensure smooth

Figure 1.1   Building a Smoother Path

Consistency results from combining return streams that are reliably different

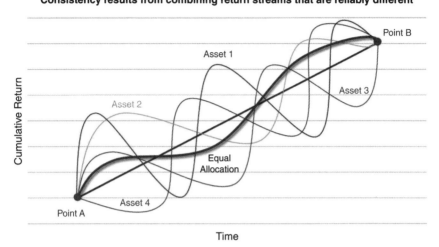

operation for the whole. If you were to view the inside of a properly designed and constructed engine block, you would observe chaos as various pieces would be operating in different directions and at a varying pace. Yet, the finely tuned machine purrs along smoothly when viewed from the outside. I believe we can build portfolios using a similar construct.

Ray famously referred to this investment approach as "the holy grail." If investors are able to identify 10 good, uncorrelated investments and split their portfolio roughly equally among them, then they could enjoy attractive returns with low risk. The concept is supported by the notion that when one investment is doing well, another may be underperforming, and they can balance each other out to yield a return closer to the average of the two. Including more uncorrelated return streams would drastically reduce the total risk of the portfolio.

The simple math is extremely compelling. A portfolio of a single risky asset with an 8% expected return and 15% volatility (standard deviation) has about a 30% chance of losing money in a single year. If we have five assets that offer the same returns and risk but are uncorrelated with one another and we allocate equally across the five, then the risk of the total portfolio is *less than half* of the one-asset portfolio, and the odds of losing money in a single year significantly lower. Risk decreases even further as we go from five uncorrelated assets to 10, although there are diminishing returns to diversification beyond a certain point. The math is provided in Table 1.1.

Table 1.1   Portfolios of High Returning, Uncorrelated Investments

	1-Asset Portfolio	5-Asset Portfolio	10-Asset Portfolio
Return	8%	8%	8%
Risk (volatility)	15%	7%	5%
Odds of losing money in one year	30%	12%	5%

Same Return and Less Risk –>

As Figure 1.1 and Table 1.1 illustrate, a similar return can be mathematically achieved with less risk *if* lowly correlated, high-returning assets are utilized to construct a portfolio.

Finding 5 to 10 uncorrelated investments with attractive returns can be difficult, particularly in liquid public markets (which is the scope of this study). However, the point of this exercise is to demonstrate the power of diversification and the simple approach that we follow to construct a portfolio with expected returns competitive with equities with less risk. Clearly, implementing the conceptual framework can be challenging, which is why I have devoted an entire book to the subject. We now dive one step deeper into the risk parity framework by describing where returns come from, defining risk, and explaining why a traditional portfolio is poorly balanced.

THE SOURCE OF RETURNS

Investors have a choice when deciding how to allocate their portfolio. The safest bet is to leave all the money in cash and earn a guaranteed rate of return. The return is based on the prevailing interest rate at the time. You can think of the rate offered by a bank in a savings account or in insured certificates of deposit (CDs) as examples. Money market funds are also considered very low risk investments that provide interest payments without risk of principal. The Federal Reserve of the United States effectively sets the rate of cash. Over time, cash rates have fluctuated as the economic environment has shifted. In the early 1980s, cash yields were over 10% and as of this writing in 2021, they are closer to 0%.

Investors who seek higher returns than cash, have the option to take greater risk (which will be defined next) with their assets. In order to be enticed to purchase investments with safe cash, various asset classes should offer a return premium over cash. In other words, unless you expected to earn a reasonable excess return above cash over time by taking risk, you would not take the risk. This "risk premium" can be observed by measuring the long-term performance difference between risky investments and cash. For example, since 1926 the stock market has outpaced cash by about 5% per annum.

In general, asset classes that are riskier have delivered greater excess returns than those that are less risky. This should make sense since investors should pay attention to the level of compensation for a certain level of risk. Why would I take a lot of risk to earn just a little more return? As a result, historical asset-class returns and risk are somewhat proportional: those with greater risk offer higher expected returns than those with less risk.

My ultimate goal in this book is to walk through an efficient way to capture the risk premiums available in various asset classes. That is, we wish to identify the best way to seek better returns than cash by investing in a diverse set of asset classes while minimizing risk. In fact, we seek returns much better than cash and want to be thoughtful about how to achieve this objective without taking undue risk.

It is important to note that there is no attempt to predict what the future economic environment may look like or which asset classes will be the best performers over the next market cycle. We want to be, by and large, indifferent to what environment transpires next and how it may shift through time. We are trying to identify a thoughtful, neutral portfolio that can stand the test of time through a passive long-term allocation without the need for tactical decision-making. In fact, the design of this balanced allocation assumes that the future twists and turns of the markets are inherently difficult to anticipate in advance. This is why it makes sense to maintain a well-diversified portfolio at all times.

WHAT IS RISK?

The rate of return of an investment is a relatively straightforward notion to understand. You invest $100 and in one year your portfolio is worth $110. This means you earned a 10% return. Risk, on the other hand, is multifaceted and more challenging to observe and measure. I think of risk across three different dimensions:

1. Volatility
2. Probability of catastrophic loss
3. Odds of an extended period of poor returns

Volatility is the standard measure of risk in the investment industry. The technical metric is standard deviation, which is a statistical figure of the dispersion of an investment's price change around its average over time. The more the price fluctuates around its average return, the greater the volatility. In general, a lower volatility is preferred over a higher volatility for the same return because the odds of actually earning the average return improve. This is because investors are less likely to get in and out at inopportune times.

A major shortcoming of the volatility metric is that a return stream can exhibit reasonable volatility most of the time, but suddenly experience a major loss of capital. That is, the average may be acceptable yet understate extreme negative outcomes. Many experts have commented that highly improbable results seem to occur far more frequently than statistically expected. In other words, the notorious "100-year flood" seems to hit financial markets far more often than once every 100 years. We've witnessed firsthand some of these outliers in the last three decades alone, with the 1999 tech bubble and bust, the 2008 global financial crisis, and the 2020 global pandemic. For this reason, the probability of a catastrophic loss should also be analyzed when considering the risk of a strategy.

Last, a longer-term perspective of risk is justified. Consider that the volatility and distribution may be acceptable, but the average return could be low for an extended period of time. That is, the odds of poor returns over a long period (e.g., the so-called lost decade in 1990s Japan) may be the most relevant risk. After all, investors may be able to live through the roller-coaster ride associated with a precipitous drop and subsequent rebound, but 10 years of severe underperformance may be difficult to overcome. This is particularly relevant for investors who rely on a certain rate of return to fund annual expenses.

A well-balanced portfolio should be structured to minimize all three aforementioned risks for a desired long-term return objective. All three risks are pertinent and worth consideration because each can have a material negative impact on investors.

THE 60/40 PORTFOLIO IS NOT WELL-BALANCED

The conventional "balanced" portfolio is made up of 60% stocks and 40% intermediate-term bonds. This allocation is commonly used in finance books and the media as a representation of a typical portfolio. In fact, there are hundreds of professionally managed strategies that benchmark to the 60/40 portfolio and use "balanced" in their title. However, a simple high-level risk analysis using the definition just presented will reveal that the 60/40 portfolio is actually very poorly balanced.

The 60/40 portfolio scores poorly across the three dimensions of risk just described. The level of volatility is greater than necessary for the expected return. This point will become more apparent when I describe the risk parity portfolio later in the book. This conventional balanced allocation is also prone to significant losses and long stretches of under-performance, since its returns are almost entirely dependent on the stock market, which serves as the core return driver. A statistic that surprises many investors is that a 60/40 portfolio is over 95% correlated to a 100% equity allocation. For instance, the 60/40 portfolio experienced steep declines along with equities during the first quarter of 2020 (–12%) and during the Global Financial Crisis of 2008–2009 (–35%), and it grossly underperformed most investors' objectives during the entire decade of the 2000s (earning less than 3% per year and falling slightly behind cash over 10 years) as global stocks suffered negative returns for 10 years. Regardless, few practitioners raise concerns about the lack of balance in the 60/40 portfolio, and even fewer argue that the typical "balanced fund" is effectively engaged in false advertising.

In my experience, most investors don't really appreciate what diversification means. There appears to be an overemphasis on the number of line items as opposed to how diversifying each investment is relative to other holdings. They may think that they are diversifying by allocating to assets with slightly different characteristics or to funds with different managers (e.g., US small-cap equities, US large-cap, Vanguard, Fidelity, etc.), but all of those allocations tend to be highly correlated to each other. In other words, the differences many investors focus on are largely immaterial. As a result, they allocate to assets that all behave more or less the same way and barely diversify each other at all.

If the 60/40 portfolio is so poorly balanced, then how did it become the conventional balanced portfolio? A description of how this allocation evolved to become the convention and the thought process that backs its construction is warranted. The logic makes perfect sense, which explains why it has prevailed, and its place atop the balanced hierarchy has rarely been challenged.

We must go back to the story of Ray and his view that the starting point for most people is where others left off as opposed to a full reexamination of the central assumptions. When investors look to build a portfolio, they consider a menu of options. The typical choices include various equity and fixed income segments, because stocks and bonds represent the backbone of finance. Companies generally issue equity or debt to raise capital, and investors have the opportunity to own a piece of each in order to participate in the prosperity of the global economy. Throw in a strong bull market over the past decade and a remarkable run for both asset classes during the 1980s and 1990s as interest rates declined, and we can see why stocks and bonds as core menu options have persisted for so long.

Stocks offer high expected returns with high risk. Traditional fixed income such as intermediate-duration government and high-quality corporate bonds have lower anticipated returns with lower risk. With these two choices, investors can scale the risk of their portfolio up and down by adjusting the allocation between these two major asset classes. Those who have a high threshold for risk and/or a long time horizon may opt for 100% stocks, whereas investors who are more concerned about protecting principal may go all the way to 100% bonds. Nearly everyone will fall somewhere in between these two extremes, with the typical investor allocating 60% to stock and 40% to bonds because the risk level of that mix appears palatable for the majority.

The 60/40 portfolio has an expected return somewhere between stocks and bonds. An increase in equities above 60% yields a higher expected return, with a maximum long-term return achieved at 100% equities. A reduction in stocks below 60% lowers the return projection all the way down to the estimate for bonds for risk-averse investors who own 100% fixed income. The risk of these portfolios also scales up and down commensurate with the target return level. With this menu of choices, this is a very reasonable way to manage a portfolio.

A commonly used shorthand for determining the right allocation is to take 100 minus your age and allocate that amount to equities, with the remainder going to bonds. Following that rule of thumb, a 70-year-old should put 30% in stocks, while a 30-year-old, who has more time to ride the ups and downs of the stock market, can accept the greater risk that comes with a 70% equity portfolio as compensation for the higher long-term return. If you're 30 and saving for retirement, there's a good argument to invest a majority of your portfolio in stocks *if you're limited to these options*. Although professional advisors may debate the percentages, few would argue with this general framework. The problem is that this logical sequence leads investors down a path that often results in poorly balanced portfolios that take unnecessary risk.

RISK PARITY FRAMEWORK OVERVIEW

Investors have the opportunity to build a much more efficient allocation: one that seeks higher returns with lower risk. The breakthrough comes from expanding the menu of available investments and evaluating the asset allocation decision through a different approach. These additional asset classes are very well known; have long histories; and are supported by extremely large, public, liquid markets. They have simply been ignored because of a lack of independent analysis and a dogged herd mentality. By completely reassessing the investment options, we are taking the critical step espoused by Ray of not starting at the same point as others but commencing at the most fundamental level.

Risk parity approaches the investment problem of earning high returns while minimizing risk from a completely different vantage point from that embraced by most investment professionals. We strive for what may seem impossible when viewing the task through the conventional lens and utilizing the traditional tools. In this book, I apply a basic two-step process to answer the following question:

How can we build a simple, passively managed portfolio that can outperform equities over the long run with less risk?

We must begin from a blank slate and without regard to conventional wisdom, which many would immediately respond with a resounding "no way!" to the question posed. In the first step, we select from the appropriate asset classes that will enable us to construct an extremely well diversified portfolio that exhibits moderate risk. This involves focusing on assets that reliably perform differently in varying economic environments. The environmental bias is the emphasis in this step since that is the main driver of asset-class returns.

In the second step, we structure each asset class included in our portfolio to earn high returns competitive with equities over the long run. Many investors may be astounded by the ease in which we can boost the expected return of certain asset classes that are traditionally considered to be low returning. By taking these steps, we are able to build a total portfolio that can outperform stocks over the long run with much less risk. In the next chapter we will dive into these steps in detail.

Note that the objective in this book is to describe the rationale for constructing a well-diversified balanced portfolio that is designed to serve as a reasonable allocation for a long-term investment. The mix does not factor in any views of what the future may hold or the current valuation of any market segment. Our risk parity portfolio is an expression of an efficient neutral allocation that is designed to weather inevitable and unexpected storms.

PEER GROUP RISK

There is one additional form of risk that is worth mentioning: peer risk. The three dimensions of risk (volatility, material loss, and an extended period of poor returns) are absolute in nature. Because of the two steps taken, (1) select diverse asset classes, and (2) structure asset classes to have equity-like returns, the absolute risk is manageable. However, the bigger risk of adopting a risk parity approach is underperformance relative to the conventional mix. In other words, if the reference point is how the strategy is doing relative to how others are invested, then the risk of underperformance can be meaningful. After all, there is always the potential of falling behind by investing differently from others. This is sometimes called peer group risk in institutional investing and also holds true for individuals who compare themselves to peers and how the market is performing. I mention this because I have been using this investment approach for decades and have observed that one of the greatest challenges in holding on is living through periods of relative underperformance.

CHAPTER TWO

Two Steps to Build a Well-Balanced Portfolio

While I was on my journey to determine the optimal portfolio, one that could stand the test of time, Bridgewater introduced me to a conceptual discovery that provided a philosophical breakthrough. The traditional thought process of constructing a diversified portfolio joins two core concepts into one: risk and return. Equities have high risk and high return, while traditional intermediate-term bonds have low risk and low return. When viewed through a conventional lens, these two options force the investor to have to choose between risk and return by deciding how much to invest in high-returning stocks versus low-returning but safer bonds. Accepting greater risk results in higher returns over time, and accepting less risk results in lower returns. There is a well-established and, in many ways, commonsense compromise that you can't expect higher returns without taking more risk and you can't expect lower risk if you seek higher returns.

A simple shift in investment approach can completely change the logical path that can be followed to arrive at a more ideal portfolio solution. From a high level, there are two fundamental steps:

1. Which asset classes should we own to *reduce risk*?
2. How do we structure each asset class to get an *equity-like return*?

We can consider risk and return separately. First, we should explore how to build an allocation of highly diverse asset classes to manage risk (without concern for the returns of those asset classes). By removing the return constraint and focusing purely on risk mitigation, we can open up the universe of viable options to maximize diversification. After we have identified the appropriate assets in which to invest, then we can structure each to have an acceptable expected return.

The goal of this chapter is to introduce this new perspective by first providing an overview of the conceptual framework. I will attempt to keep the discussion high-level in the remainder of this chapter to lay out the roadmap. The following chapters will dive into each component with greater detail.

STEP 1: WHICH ASSET CLASSES TO REDUCE RISK?

There are a wide variety of asset classes within public markets that are readily available to investors. I had previously mentioned the traditional asset classes of equities and intermediate-term government and high-quality corporate bonds that make up the conventional 60/40 mix. Other popular market segments include lower-quality, higher-yielding bonds (which have come into favor as interest rates on high quality bonds have dropped to historic lows), cash (as a safe-haven asset), and real estate (something that can appreciate like stocks but offers income like bonds).

To determine the appropriate assets to incorporate into our risk parity portfolio, I will begin the logical sequence at the most fundamental starting point rather than work off the traditional menu of choices. We will also ignore the conventional thought process for developing a portfolio that involves scaling up and down risk by allocating more or less to equities versus less risky bonds. In short, I am asking you to temporarily suspend any preconceived notions about building a properly diversified portfolio so we can start from a blank slate.

The main objective of constructing a well-balanced portfolio is to produce a steady return with low risk of catastrophic loss and low odds of an extended period of underperformance. To begin, a core understanding is that the manner in which the economic environment unfolds is the biggest influence on asset-class prices. This appreciation is essential because it will inform how we go about selecting the appropriate assets to include in our portfolio. Approaching the question from this angle makes sense since we are trying to build balance, and recognizing the key drivers of asset-class returns is essential to that process. This lines up directly with our goals of controlling downside risk and minimizing the odds of a long stretch of poor results. Notice from the start that viewing the problem through this lens greatly differs from the traditional method used to develop the appropriate asset allocation.

The Economic Environment Drives Asset-Class Returns

Imagine that you own a small private business that develops and sells a product. Would you generally expect sales to improve or decline during an economic collapse like 2008 or the first quarter of 2020? Unless you sell something extremely unique, most would answer that a material economic downturn is probably an unfavorable environment for your business. Likewise, if we are in the middle of a prosperous period and business is booming, you should reasonably expect the value of your venture to increase. What if your expenses unexpectedly spike due to rising inflation and you are unable to fully pass through the increase to your customers? Wouldn't it make sense that the value of your profits would be negatively impacted, and the opposite would be true if your input costs declined?

The stock market works the exact same way and is supported by an identical rationale. A stock represents an ownership stake in a public company. The stock market is simply made up of a large basket of individual stocks and provides a broad representation of public company performance. The main difference between a public stock and your private business is that the former trades on a stock exchange and its value is correspondingly fully transparent on a daily basis. Anyone can transact in a share of the stock, and the market of potential buyers and sellers sets the prevailing price, which is largely based on the knowledge of the public. The consensus ultimately establishes the fair market value of the business according to its perceived value, which, just like your business, is heavily influenced by the economic environment. This is why the stock market plunged 33% in five weeks during the onset of COVID-19. Investors were justifiably terrified that revenues would fall off a cliff as the economy was shut down. Even though you may not have perceived the value of your private business to have similarly declined because its price is not published every second, you would have likely suffered a similar fate at that time.

If we look deeper into why the value fluctuates based on the economic environment, we see that each business can be viewed as a series of future cash flows. Today's value of the business is based on the market expectation of the value of the stream of cash it will distribute in the future. The distributions are dependent on the revenues of the business as well as its expenses, which together determine the net profit to owners.

When investors buy stock, they exchange safe cash for a risky investment in a company because of the expectation of excess returns above cash in the form of future cash flows (to compensate for the risk). The price paid discounts future economic expectations of growth and inflation, since those two factors have a material impact on the stream of cash flows. This connection between shifts in growth and inflation and individual asset-class performance will be fully described in the following chapters. You will see how each asset class (such as stocks, Treasuries, and commodities) has a different bias to different growth and inflation outcomes.

Of course, a single business's cash flows are more likely to exhibit idiosyncratic factors specific to its revenues and expenses. If your private business provides software solutions and the cause of the economic downturn is a global pandemic, then your revenues could soar, whereas a travel agency may not be as fortunate. However, when we take the entire stock market in aggregate, the unique aspects to each business net out, and the overall economic environment becomes the primary driver of returns.

Importantly, when we refer to rising and falling growth and inflation, we should think of it relative to what was originally discounted. In other words, if the market expects and is priced for 3% growth and we get 1% growth, then that is a negative influence on assets biased to do well when growth is improving, even though the economy grew. Buyers and sellers agreed on a price level that factored in 3% growth and only received 1%. Therefore, the price discounted more growth than actually transpired. Once the knowledge of the lower growth rate gets recognized, then the value of the market declines, all else being equal, to reflect this lower growth. Since current and future expected cash flows are now lower than previously thought, this means, practically, that businesses are now worth less than they used to be, since they are expected to produce lower profits. Prices adjust to reflect this shift. Changes in inflation work the same way.

Shifts in growth and inflation heavily influence the returns of other asset classes as well. Treasuries, for instance, move inversely with interest rates: as rates rise, Treasuries underperform, and they outperform as rates fall. Interest rates are the key tool used by the Federal Reserve (the "Fed"), which is the central bank of the United States; other major economies around the world have their own central banks. The Fed uses interest rates to manage the economy. During weakening growth and/or falling inflation periods, interest rates are reduced, which increases the present value of Treasuries' fixed future cash flows. When growth or inflation rises, the Fed increases interest rates, reducing the value of those future cash flows discounted back to the present at the higher rate. There is a fundamental link between economic shifts and the price of Treasuries, which are biased to do well when the economy weakens and/or inflation is falling. Beyond the impact of Fed tightening/easing, changes in inflation/growth expectations affect asset prices directly. If inflation rises, lenders will demand a higher interest rate to ensure they earn a real return, and borrowers will be eager to borrow at prevailing lower rates knowing they can repay their debts in cash that's worth less tomorrow than it is today. This pushes up the market interest rate to a new equilibrium between borrowers and lenders.

Similarly, if growth is very strong, demand for capital will increase from borrowers eager to build or expand their businesses. Greater demand to borrow also pushes up interest rates, just as rates decline when growth weakens and demand for capital falls.

Treasury Inflation-Protected Securities (TIPS) are similar to Treasuries in that they are government-guaranteed bonds and can serve as a safe-haven asset. They differ from Treasuries in that they are directly linked to inflation, because these securities pay the holder the prevailing inflation rate as measured by the consumer price index (CPI). Therefore, TIPS are biased to outperform in the exact opposite environment of equities – namely, falling growth and rising inflation. They are also a good diversifier versus Treasuries even though TIPS and Treasuries are both government bonds. The latter outperforms during falling inflationary periods and does poorly when inflation rises since it receives a fixed interest rate as opposed to an inflation pass through.

Commodities are another diversifying asset class. We can break commodities down into two subgroups: industrial commodities and gold. Industrial commodities include energy, industrial metals, and agriculture, which are considered good inflation hedges. This is because higher commodity prices are actually one component of general price inflation since they are a key input into many goods and services, and are literally part of the CPI measure. Gold, on the other hand, is more of a currency and a storehold of wealth. Its price is far less influenced by aggregate demand as an input to produce something else. Consequently, the economic bias of industrial commodities is to outperform in *rising* growth and rising inflation environments whereas gold is more of a *falling* growth, rising inflation asset. It also serves as a useful diversifier against more extreme growth and inflation environments and periods of crisis. The year 2008 and the first quarter 2020 offer good examples of the divergence: gold rallied in both periods, while industrial commodities collapsed amid the severe economic downturn.

I have devoted a single chapter to each major asset class to provide greater insight into the relationships between the environment and returns, so I won't get into too much detail here. Most important, all the cause-effect linkages are logical and reliable and can be supported by long-term data. With an appreciation of how each asset class is biased to perform in various economic environments, we can thoughtfully select the appropriate asset classes to include in our balanced portfolio.

Four Diverse Asset Classes

There are numerous asset classes to pick from. The key question is how we can take advantage of diversification across various asset classes to reduce risk. Our goal isn't to select or weight them based on return or risk but based on how they diversify each other (i.e., what drives their performance). The core observation is that asset classes have two key drivers in common – growth and inflation – and what distinguishes them from each other is how they respond to those drivers.

Based on this logical sequence and our desire to build a well-diversified portfolio, the next natural step is to select a group of assets that perform differently from each other because they respond differently to changes in growth and inflation. By temporarily ignoring the returns and risks of various asset classes (in contrast to the way most people think about building a portfolio), the steps should seem reasonable and, in many ways, very obvious.

There are four general economic environments that should be considered: rising growth, falling growth, rising inflation, and falling inflation. There are four asset classes that cover these economic outcomes:

1. **Global equities** – rising growth, falling inflation
2. **Commodities** – rising inflation
   a. **Industrial commodities** – rising growth
   b. **Gold** – falling growth
3. **Treasuries** – falling growth, falling inflation
4. **TIPS** – falling growth, rising inflation

You may notice that some commonly used asset classes like intermediate-term core fixed income, high-yield bonds, and real estate investment trusts (REITs) were excluded from our list. I believe Treasuries are a better environmental fit for falling growth than core fixed income because their higher credit quality means they will typically outperform during extreme adverse environments like 2008 and first quarter 2020. High-yield bonds have the same bias as equities (rising growth, falling inflation) since their returns are largely driven by changes in creditworthiness, so they don't add much incremental benefit from a diversification standpoint. You'll see later when we discuss returns that they also have a lower return profile and are less tax efficient than equities, which is another reason to exclude them. REITs also are similar to equities in terms of how they respond to shifting economic environments. This one is a closer call because real estate is a real asset and has some inflation-hedging components. However, real estate is often purchased with debt, which makes it sensitive to rising interest rates, and rents can often lag inflation – particularly with fixed, longer-term leases. Therefore, it has historically not provided as reliable and consistent an inflation hedge as TIPS and commodities, which are included in our mix of assets.

STEP 2: HOW TO STRUCTURE EACH ASSET CLASS TO HAVE EQUITY-LIKE RETURNS

The first step was to select a diverse set of asset classes that are biased to perform differently in varying economic environments. This creates the potential to reduce risk, since the positive performance of assets that do well in a given environment can offset the negative performance of assets that do poorly. Thus far, we have not discussed returns, because we separated out risk reduction from return maximization at the outset. By isolating the key drivers of asset-class returns, we can follow a relatively straightforward logical sequence to arrive at the asset classes selected for our portfolio.

We can now turn to the second step that will enable us to design the selected asset classes to deliver an expected return competitive with stocks over the long run. One problem that investors face is that some of the diversifying assets are low returning. This apparent obstacle commonly turns investors away from investing in many of the most diverse asset classes. However, this is a problem that can be easily solved.

Importantly, investors are not forced to take the chosen asset classes in the packages in which they are typically offered. For instance, Treasuries and TIPS are normally considered low-risk, low-return asset classes. Commodities are also often thought to be lower returning than equities. *Fortunately, we can take simple steps to structure each asset class to offer a long-term expected return competitive with equities.* I appreciate that the preceding italicized statement may sound unreasonable, counterintuitive, and possibly too good to be true (which is precisely why I emphasized it). Imagine for a moment if Treasuries, TIPS, and commodities could be held in a way that would offer equity-like returns over the long run. You could see the power of a portfolio that is balanced across a reliably diverse set of asset classes, each of which would be expected to earn returns comparable to equities. With these asset classes, we should be able to achieve attractive returns while minimizing risk. Furthermore, all of this is possible without any reliance on active management. A simple passive portfolio can outperform even a 100% equity allocation over the long run.

This is where the "parity" component of risk parity is relevant. Parity refers to the state of being equal. Within the context of building portfolios using a risk parity framework, we take the major step of increasing the risk in each asset class so that it has a roughly equal long-term expected return as equities. Since most asset classes have a comparable return-to-risk ratio, this step basically involves equalizing the risk of various asset classes to raise the expected return to the level of stocks. Using long-term volatility as a measure of asset-class risk, we can now consider a wide range of investment options to create a diversified portfolio. Equalizing the risk to synthetically create long-term equity-like expected returns across multiple and diverse asset classes brings us closer to the smoother path described at the beginning of this book. By limiting our universe of investment options to those that are not correlated yet high returning, we eliminate the need to have to choose between low- and high-returning assets like those in a 60/40 framework.

Years ago, I had a conversation with a highly successful investor. He had earned a PhD in Economics from the Booth School of Business at the University of Chicago, one of the most prestigious and well-respected business schools in the world. He was well trained in portfolio management and had over 30 years of experience with investing. He would easily qualify as a sophisticated investor by any measure. I asked him a simple question: if you were investing for 50 years and had to construct a portfolio that consists of stocks and bonds that you couldn't change, how would you allocate between the two? His quick and confident response of 100% stocks because everyone knows that stocks beat bonds over the long run was not a surprise. If I posed the same query to 100 people with his background and expertise, I would likely receive the same answer the majority of the time, if not every time.

His response was expected, but my rebuttal completely caught him off guard. "Why would you say 100% stocks when the two asset classes have about the same return over the long run?" I added, "why wouldn't you split them 50/50 since you can get a similar return with much less risk?" He was puzzled. I clarified my point by explaining that bonds could easily be structured to have similar return and risk as equities with some leverage and did not have to be held in their conventional form. I spent a few minutes describing that the only reason bonds are considered to have lower returns than stocks is that they are less risky, and that characteristic can be easily adjusted. I shared some long-term data to back my point. He said that in his 30 years in the business no one had ever brought up this idea to him because stocks beat bonds over the long run was such a basic assumption that it was beyond reproach. In short order, he restated his answer as 50/50 and was amazed at how quickly and easily a core tenet that he had assumed to be a fundamental investment truth for decades was disaffirmed.

We can do the same thing for other asset classes. That is, we can structure multiple asset classes to have equity-like returns by adjusting their risk to match equities. Hence, the origin of the term *risk parity*. We adjust the risk of various assets to match equities so we can equalize their long-term return expectations. This step in our process involves essentially creating a new menu from which to select investments. Risk can be equalized either by employing some leverage or by choosing prepackaged ways to access certain asset classes. In the next several chapters, I will address each asset class individually, devoting a single chapter to each included in our risk parity portfolio: equities, Treasuries, TIPS, and commodities. In each chapter I will describe in detail how to structure each to earn equity-like returns over the long run.

Putting It All Together

By going through the process of selecting a diverse set of asset classes biased to outperform in different economic environments, we can mitigate the risk of our portfolio. By structuring each of these assets to have similar returns and risk as equities, we can raise the expected return of the portfolio to be competitive with equities. The combination of the two steps results in an extremely well balanced portfolio that exhibits much less risk than equities and offers high expected returns. It really is as simple as that.

In the following chapters I will walk you through a more detailed analysis of each of these asset classes and how to structure them to have comparable long-term expected returns as equities. I will also cover additional asset classes that I excluded and the rationale for doing so. Our specific risk parity portfolio including the final allocation to each asset class will be devised as I progress through the logical sequence established to this point. I will support the allocation and conceptual framework with very long-term returns through varying environments. I will end with implementation strategies and a description of the periods during which the risk parity portfolio could be expected to underperform.

CHAPTER THREE

Equities

When people ask how the market did today, they are undoubtedly referring to the stock market, even though there are many markets to consider. The vast majority of headlines, analyses, and conversations are about how the stock market is faring. Bonds, commodities, and real estate are just a few of many other major markets that do not seem to receive the same attention as stocks. For some reason our nation is gripped by the stock market.

Consequently, equities are a staple in nearly every portfolio. Those that are well balanced, as well as the imbalanced variety, are certain to contain some allocation to public companies. Thus, for most investors, equities do not require a compelling argument for their inclusion in portfolios (unlike several of the other asset classes that will be covered later). In fact, most investors start with the assumption that they should own as high a proportion of equities as they can handle because stocks offer the highest expected return of the major asset classes. Then, bonds and other assets are added to fill the remainder and lower the overall volatility of the portfolio. This is a flawed premise, even though it's where most investors start. As discussed before, stocks do not offer a higher expected return than other asset classes because any asset class can be structured to deliver similar expected returns to stocks.

My main aim in this chapter is to emphasize the need to evaluate the equity allocation decision from a different perspective. You should think about it in terms of balance. Treat the equity decision the same as you

21

would the other asset classes. Ask in what economic environments are they biased to outperform and how do they fit within a balanced portfolio framework.

WHAT ARE STOCKS?

An investment in a stock represents an equity ownership in a public company. This is why stocks are also referred to as equities. If you buy Apple stock, for example, you instantly become a part owner of Apple. As an owner of the company, you benefit from the company's current and future expected profits, which are reflected in the price of the stock. When profits surprise to the upside, the stock price rises, and vice versa. Apple is one company. The broad stock market consists of a large basket of publicly traded companies like Apple.

HOW DO STOCKS PERFORM ACROSS DIFFERENT ENVIRONMENTS?

In the previous chapter, I summarized the economic bias of equities as rising growth and falling inflation. I dive deeper into the explanation for these particular sensitivities in this chapter. The goal is to demonstrate the logic that supports this understanding since that is what provides an enduring, reliable appreciation for how equities may do in future economic periods.

Growth/Inflation Bias: Conceptual Framework

Economic growth refers to changes in real gross domestic product (GDP), which is an inflation-adjusted measure of the value of all goods and services an economy produces. Real GDP is a way to quantify the economic output of the economy.[1] When real GDP increases from the prior period, we consider that growth. Over time, many economies tend to grow as populations increase and/or productivity improves causing real GDP to rise. For our purposes, we are more concerned about positive and negative growth *surprises* as opposed to whether real GDP is rising or falling. The latter indicates absolute growth, whereas the former is based on how future growth transpires *relative to what was expected*. If the market anticipates that the economy will grow by 4% and it only grows by 2%, then that is a negative surprise even though growth was positive.

---

[1] https://www.investopedia.com/terms/r/realgdp.asp

A positive growth surprise is a plus for equities because it directly impacts the top-line revenues of most companies. This is due to the stronger economic activity that has led to increased spending. More spending results in higher company revenues since someone's spending is someone else's income. Higher revenues, all else being equal, produce greater profits for corporations. Better-than-expected profits generate upward pressure on stock prices since ultimately a company's profits are what make a company worth something. When the economy grows faster than discounted, this logical sequence typically leads to higher equity prices because the old price did not reflect the improved conditions. As a result, equity prices are impacted by unexpected shifts in economic growth. When growth comes in better than conditions already discounted in the stock price, then a positive influence results. The opposite is also true: negative surprises generally lead to price declines.

There are two parts of the profit equation: revenues and expenses. Rising growth positively influences revenues, whereas falling inflation can reduce expenses (depending on the nature of the company's business). Inflation is a measure of the increase in the cost of goods and services. These same items are inputs into the cost of doing business for corporations. Moreover, falling inflation exerts downward pressure on interest rates, which also benefits companies as the cost of borrowing money declines. As company costs decline (from both lower borrowing and input costs), profit margins increase, all else being equal. Thus, if growth transpires as expected and inflation falls more than expected, then revenues may come in as priced, but the margins may improve due to falling expenses. The net result is positive because profits have improved more than discounted.

Note that if growth is rising and inflation is falling simultaneously, then this outcome marks a double positive for stocks and generally yields the best overall environment for this asset class. Such an economic period largely explained the unprecedented equity returns during the 1980s and 1990s bull market. After the stagflationary 1970s, during which inflation rose and growth disappointed, the market had discounted similar results at the beginning of the 1980s. Nearly the opposite environment transpired (falling inflation and rising growth), and because of the vast divergence between what was expected and what actually happened, stocks surged.

As we walk through the various asset classes, describing their fundamental economic biases, we will cover all the various growth and inflation environments. At each step, I will enter the discussed asset class until we successfully fill in each box with an equal number of asset classes. Table 3.1 kicks us off, with equities inserted under rising growth and falling inflation.

Table 3.1   Asset-Class Economic Biases

Economic Environment	Favored Asset Classes
Rising Growth	Equities
Falling Growth	
Rising Inflation	
Falling Inflation	Equities

Growth/Inflation Bias: Historical Returns

Together, the rational cause-effect relationship between unexpected shifts in growth and inflation reliably impacts stock prices and results in price fluctuations over time. Moreover, so-called good environments characterized by rising growth or falling inflation relative to expectations generally exhibit stronger equity returns than so-called bad periods during which the opposite sets of conditions exist. Not only do the conceptual linkages make sense, but long-term historical data also support- this cause-effect relationship. The historical data backing this connection is summarized in Figure 3.1.

**Figure 3.1   Annualized Global Equity Excess Returns by Economic Environment –
January 1926 to March 2021**

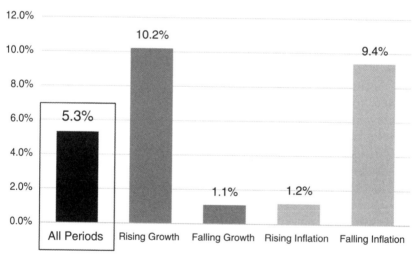

Source: Bloomberg. Methodology used to determine if growth and inflation are rising or falling: current growth or inflation rate compared to average of the trailing 12-month period. If the current rate (of growth/inflation) is higher, then that is considered a rising growth/ inflation period and vice versa. The logic is based on the observation that most people expect the future to closely resemble the recent trend line.

Note that I used "excess" returns for the performance measures in Figure 3.1 and plan to do the same in other long-term historical comparisons. The term *excess returns* refers to the returns earned in excess of cash (or the risk-free rate). This is relevant because we are most concerned with what we gain by taking risk. For example, if cash is yielding 6% (as it was in the late 1990s), then stocks returning 7% are not as attractive as when cash is yielding 0%. The difference is what truly matters. It is particularly insightful to compare excess returns as opposed to total returns when reviewing performance over long periods of time, since cash rates have been as low as 0% (since 2009) and as high as 16% (in the early 1980s).

Notice how much better equities have historically performed during good climates versus bad times. You may also recognize that the average excess return since 1926 of 5.3% is just about midway between the positive growth environment returns (10.2%) and the negative growth climate returns (1.1%). The same observation holds for falling inflation periods (9.4%) and rising inflationary environments (1.2%). The reason the average is almost exactly in the middle of the two ends of the spectrum is because of the frequency of each economic environment. This is because each economic climate occurs roughly half the time, because what really matters is how the future transpires relative to what had been expected to occur. In fact, about half of the months since 1926 can be characterized as rising growth and about half as falling growth. Rising inflation and falling inflation each also cover about half of the measured environments. This is because growth and inflation are just as likely to *surprise* on the upside as they are on the downside.

Table 3.2 summarizes the same data but broken out by decade. I also broadly describe the general economic environment and other driving factors that characterized each decade for background.

As would be expected, the worst decades (1930s, 1970s, and 2000s) were dominated by economic environments during which equities were biased to perform poorly. Conversely, the best periods (1940s, 1950s, 1980s, 1990s, and 2010s) were driven by favorable economic conditions.

Table 3.2   Equity Excess Returns by Decade

Decade	General Environment	Average Excess Returns
1930s	Depression (weak growth/deflation)	−4%
1940s	Wartime economy (borrowing/quantitative easing)	9%
1950s	Postwar economy (strong growth)	17%
1960s	Rising inflation	4%
1970s	Stagflation	−1%
1980s	Boom (rising growth/falling inflation)	8%
1990s	Roaring (rising growth/falling inflation)	6%
2000s	Tech bust, financial crisis (weak growth)	−3%
2010s	Reflation (borrowing/QE/rising growth)	9%

Source: Bloomberg.

WHAT IS THE BEST WAY TO INVEST IN EQUITIES?

The main goal of the equity allocation in our risk parity portfolio is to provide broad exposure to the asset class. Buying equities should be profitable over time as investors are compensated for taking risk. By obtaining broad diversification to this asset class, we increase the odds of capturing that risk premium over time.

At the same time, we should also seek to achieve the targeted exposure as efficiently as possible. We want low fees, low taxes, and high liquidity. Exchange-traded funds (ETFs) are a good place to start as they are generally known for providing expansive market exposure with rock-bottom expenses in a highly tax-efficient vehicle. By investing in a few ETFs, investors can gain easy access to a diversified basket of over 10,000 stocks with costs driven down to near zero (due to fierce competition by fund managers in this space).

A decision also needs to be made about the sector and country allocation within global equities. Should there be a home bias or an emphasis on a particular sector that is expected to outperform in the future? What about overweighting a growth or value orientation or perhaps focusing more on smaller or larger stocks?

My general preference for the risk parity portfolio is to avoid tilting in any particular direction since the main goal is to maintain balanced exposure to various asset classes. Within equities, I generally don't want to take an active view on any subsegment because I have far greater confidence in the benefits of proper diversification than I do in our abilities to consistently and accurately make market timing calls. It is safer to assume that the broad stock market will directionally perform a certain way during various economic outcomes than it is to guess which part of the market will outperform the average.

I also have a penchant to keep things simple, because I have often found that many investors try to get overly precise in these matters. Investing is not an exact science and, in fact, involves so many factors (many of which can be considered irrational at times) that some argue it is not a science at all. The overall concepts are compelling, whereas many of the minute details are far less important and have little impact on the big picture results over the long run as the differences tend to net out.

To keep it simple, we can split the equity portfolio equally between US and non-US stocks. Some propose following a market capitalization methodology under the assumption that the market prices of all stocks represent the value that incorporates all known public information at any point in time. This is fine as well, but, again, may not make much difference in the end. As of this writing, US stocks make up a little over half of the global market cap-weighted index, so a 50/50 approach between US and non-US stocks is a reasonable proxy anyway.

Within US stocks, a market capitalization approach works well with exposure across growth, value, and core; and small, mid, and large capitalization stocks. This allows for easy implementation using an all-capitalization US equity ETF, of which there are many to choose based on personal preference.

Outside of the United States, I like to overweight emerging markets for two reasons. First, emerging markets are riskier than non-US developed markets and so come prepackaged to have higher expected returns (to compensate investors for this added risk). The greater risk comes from the fact that they are by definition stocks domiciled in less developed economies that have greater currency, political, and legal risks. Second and related, emerging markets offer better diversification than non-US developed stocks when compared to US equities. This is also because the economic cycles of countries like China, South Korea, Taiwan, India, and Brazil (among others) tend to be different from the United States. This is in contrast to the economies of the eurozone, United Kingdom, Japan, and the rest of the developed world, which have historically been more correlated to that of the United States.

STOCK MARKET CYCLES

Stocks for the long run is a concept that has been ingrained in the psyche of investors. The unfortunate reality, however, is that the long run may be too long for most. As described earlier, good environments for equities generally occur when growth has outperformed expectations and/or inflation has come in under what was discounted. The opposite environments represent bad periods for stocks. The challenge is that the aforementioned environments can persist for very long stretches of time. History clearly bears this out.

Stocks only offer attractive average returns over the long run. Averages can be very misleading. Imagine an asset class that averages 10% per year, but only delivers positive returns once every 100 years. It earns 0% every year with the exception of once a century, when it produces a positive 1,000% return. An attractive average return is not terribly useful in this extreme example. By investing in this asset class you will most likely earn 0% regardless of the average. Obviously, stocks generate more reliable and consistent returns than indicated in this example, but the difference is probably less stark than you realize. The reality is that the stock market is highly cyclical. It enjoys great runs followed by long episodes of severe underperformance, as can be seen in Table 3.2. These prolonged periods are not just the three- to seven-year period that is commonly referred to as the full market cycle. They can last a decade or two, which by anyone's definition is a very long time. Regardless of your level of conviction about investing for the long run, an extended period of underperformance can truly test your patience. In reality, five years is a long time for most people, and it seems as if the time horizon investors define as long-term has been shrinking, not increasing, over the years. Indeed, it appears that we live in a world that demands immediate gratification. The trend certainly does not support greater patience over time. Every major market move is highlighted and exploited by the growing number of media outlets, which has made it quite challenging to try to maintain a long-term focus.

Table 3.3 provides a summary of the major long-term equity market cycles since 1926. This table breaks down the excess returns of equities into long-term periods, from peak to trough, and then back to the next peak. The main message is that there are lengthy periods of great results and drawn-out periods of near zero excess returns.

Notice the lengths of the time periods presented in the table. These are typically 10- to 20-year cycles. The up periods (1926–1929, 1948–1968, 1982–2000, and 2009–today) offer significant gains. However, the down cycles leave much to be desired. In all cases, the down legs have provided negative excess returns above cash, meaning that cash beat stocks for a long period of time lasting a decade or more. These bear markets account for 42% of the measurement periods since 1926. In other words, we have lived through secular bear markets in stocks for a little less than half of the last century. Most people miss these obvious cycles simply because they

Table 3.3   Long-Term Equity Cycles (1926–2021)

Period	Length of Cycle (Years)	Annualized Equity Excess Returns	% of Total Time
January 1926–August 1929	3.7	27.4%	4%
August 1929–February 1948	18.5	−1.5%	19%
February 1948–November 1968	20.8	12.7%	22%
November 1968–July 1982	13.7	−4.1%	14%
July 1982–March 2000	17.7	9.8%	19%
March 2000–February 2009	8.9	−8.4%	9%
February 2009–March 2021	12.1	13.2%	13%
Entire period	**95 Years**	**5.3%**	**42% of time below 0**

Source: Bloomberg and Evoke Advisors analysis.

are viewing the market too closely by focusing on three- to five-year cycles (which may feel like a long time to them).

The other important point to draw from Table 3.3 is the randomness of the cycles. The unpredictability lies in the timing of the inflection points in the cycles. The table makes it look like the transitions occur regularly and smoothly. In reality, each of these bull and bear markets contains mini market cycles within them. Thus, you really don't know if the cycle has turned until a much later point in time.

The key lesson is that the stock market goes through very long periods during which it underperforms expectations and its average long-term returns. By concluding that you can afford to take risk and then overweighting equities, you are taking a huge risk in the timing of your decision. If you happen to pick the wrong half of time, then you will likely be quite disappointed with your asset allocation decision. Would you really be willing to flip a coin to determine the outcome of your portfolio? Heads you win, and tails you lose. This is not the most prudent and rational approach, particularly since having a balanced portfolio (as will be shown later) would largely alleviate these risks.

Another way to analyze the long-term trends of the stock market through history is to observe rolling 10-year returns since 1926. If we assume that 10 years is a long time, then it would be informative to see the historical range of 10-year returns based on all the possible starting points since 1926. The percentage of time that the rolling 10-year returns were poor is also instructive. The results are presented in Table 3.4.

Based on this data, if you randomly picked a 10-year period that occurred sometime between 1926 and today, the odds that the returns you would earn from equities would fall below cash is about 18%. This means that the stock market underperformed cash for 10 years! From a probability perspective, this implies that you have about a one in five chance of picking a very bad 10-year period in which to invest in equities.

Table 3.4   10-Year Rolling Equity Excess Returns (1926–2021)

Excess Returns	% of Total Time	
10%+	19%	
8–10%	10%	
5.3–8%	20%	Above average
4–5.3%	10%	Below average
2–4%	16%	
0–2%	8%	
Less than 0%	18%	

Source: Bloomberg and Evoke Advisors analysis.

About 30–40% of the rolling 10-year periods produced returns well below the average, meaning that you likely would have been disappointed with the results. Since 10 years is a relatively long time for most people, this is a fact that should not be quickly dismissed. Ten years of underperformance is typically enough to cause significant financial pain. It is also sufficiently prolonged as to reasonably produce shifts in investor behavior. A bad year or two may be easily forgotten, but 10 years of dreadful results can leave a lasting impression and cause second thoughts about original assumptions, potentially leading to decisions with further negative consequences (such as changing your entire investment strategy near the lows).

It is also unrealistic for you to assume that you possess the prescience to avoid the bad times. You might think that you will certainly identify red flags before the fact and successfully sidestep bear markets. Your actual experience, you might argue, will likely be different from that listed in Table 3.4. The problem with this perspective is that the reality suggests exactly the opposite conclusion. That is, most investors are actually pre-disposed to *jump in*, not sell, before major bear markets. In fact, the odds of investors' overweighting stocks during the next 10-year bear market is probably greater than the straight odds would imply. This is because investors are saddled with the disadvantage of emotion. Even the most collected, rational investors are hardwired emotionally to want to do the wrong thing at the wrong time. Why does this continue to happen? The answer, in short, can be largely explained by the human motivations of fear and greed. Greed causes investors to chase returns after an upturn, while fear forces them to sell underperforming investments for worry that the poor results will continue.

The normal cycle typically repeats as follows: the stock market begins to string together impressive returns, optimism builds, and strong animal spirits develop. High returns attract capital, which pushes prices even higher. Momentum ensues and eventually causes long-time bears to succumb to the pressure of sitting on the sidelines and watching friends achieve great investment success with little effort. During the late stages of these long-term bull markets, manias can form and fundamentals may be largely ignored while talk of "this time is different" dominates. Widespread overconfidence, significant risk taking, excess leverage, and unrealistic expectations about the future, or all four, often signal that the end is near.

Fear begins when markets turn for the worse, often without suffi-cient warning. Just as was the case on the upside, recent returns are extrapolated into the future as hope of a market rebound fades. Funda-mentals once again become important, and risk tolerance reverts to the opposite extreme. Risk takers and highly leveraged investors are punished as too many investors try to squeeze through the exits. Prices suffer, and a long-term bear market has begun. The excesses are slowly worked off, often in conjunction with supportive monetary and/or fiscal policy, until the market becomes attractive once again, just before the inception of the next bull market (which has tended to coincide with widespread pessimism about future prospects).

This may sound like an oversimplification. However, since these long-term periods tend to last as long as 15–20 years, there is enough time between bull and bear markets for investors to forget their mistakes and fall into the same traps over and over again. In reality, these long-term periods include various shorter-term bull and bear markets within them, which makes them even more difficult to distinguish.

A recent example of these cycles will perhaps resonate with you. The last set of 10-year rolling periods during which equities earned a negative excess return occurred in the period beginning 1998 to 2000 (therefore ending from 2008 to 2010). You may recall the level of general optimism during the dot-com Internet boom. In fact, it was a time marked by substantial exuberance over the forward-looking prospects of the economy and the stock market. Many investors loaded up on stocks that promised to grow to the sky. That period may have marked one of the peaks in US infatuation with the stock market.

ARE THERE EXTRAORDINARY ENVIRONMENTS TO CONSIDER?

Deflationary environments can be absolutely devastating for equities. Deflation is vastly different from disinflation, which is what we are normally talking about when referring to falling inflation. Disinflation means that inflation is falling but not negative. It is just a smaller positive number. For instance, inflation used to be 3% and now it is 1%. But that still indicates that prices are rising by 1% per year. Deflation, in contrast, describes an environment during which inflation is actually negative. This is a relatively rare occurrence in modern financial history, but it does happen.

When we say that equities are biased to perform well during falling inflation, that comment does not apply to deflation. If inflation falls too much and dips into negative territory, then equities are not only biased to underperform, but they could lose the majority of their value in a short period of time.

During the Great Depression, which is the most significant period of deflation in US history, US stocks fell 86% in value, and it took about a quarter century and a world war to get back to even. Timing the down-turn can be quite challenging as well. It is easy to mistake a drop accompa-nied by a gloomy outlook (like what we witnessed in 2008 or first quarter 2020) as a buy-on-the-dip opportunity. Most of the time, we experience a rebound, and buying low works out to produce outsized gains. However, if a depression actually prevails, then investing after a drawdown is more akin to catching a falling knife than finding a bargain. By doubling down on the way to a complete collapse, losses can be magnified, and investors can lose far more than implied by the actual peak to trough percentage decline. More recently, we were dangerously close to such an outcome amid the 2008 Global Financial Crisis. Were it not for extraordinary pol-icy responses by the Federal Reserve and fiscal authorities, most US stock investors could have very well lost the vast majority of their wealth.

The reason for the disaster in equity prices during deflationary peri-ods can be summarized as follows: deflation is not good for an economy, even though you might argue that you would prefer to pay less for what you buy. The reason deflation is such a negative outcome is because of the vicious cycle to which it normally leads. The economy is a system that vitally depends on increased spending. The more spending there is, the better the economy, since spending improves incomes and provides for a virtuous, self-reinforcing cycle. When there is deflation, people tend to reduce their spending. This is particularly true when deflation becomes entrenched for an extended period of time. Imagine if you anticipated that prices would be lower next month than present levels. Wouldn't you most likely wait to make that big-ticket purchase at the lower price? A short-term drop in overall prices of goods and services is fine because spending would likely continue, if not pick up, as consumers take advan-tage of sale prices. However, the longer deflationary conditions exist, the greater the negative impact on spending patterns as people start to realize that they would benefit from postponing their purchases. The problem with this reaction is that, when the majority simultaneously cut spend-ing, falling incomes result, which then leads to reduced spending. This negative spiral is difficult to break and can lead an economy into a major prolonged depression. The Japanese economy since the early 1990s pro-vides a prime example of this dynamic, as does the US Great Depression in the early 1930s.

The way to somewhat protect your portfolio against this adverse out-come is by maintaining a globally diversified equity portfolio that includes exposure to economies that may not suffer a similar downturn at the same time. That said, realistically, if the United States goes into a deflationary depression, then most of the rest of the world will probably go down too.

More importantly, owning deflation hedges such as Treasuries and gold, that may actually appreciate concurrent with the equity drop, may offer the best defense. I will cover these two market segments in the next few chapters, with Treasuries coming up next.

SUMMARY

Stocks are the favored asset class and the most understood and widely covered. Most investors recognize that stocks have earned attractive long-term returns and appreciate the risk inherent in this asset class. I hope the perspective offered in this chapter helps you think of equities in a different context. Just like the other asset classes that I will cover over the next few chapters, stocks should be thought of as a valuable component of a well-balanced portfolio. Most critically, you should view equities as a return stream that has an inherent bias to perform well or poorly during particular economic environments. When observing the stock market through this lens, the long-term return cycles through which equities have fluctuated should make more sense. It is this understanding that will help you appreciate the benefits of including other asset classes in your portfolio to achieve better balance.

CHAPTER FOUR

◆

Treasuries

In Chapter 3, I covered the most popular and widely owned asset class, equities. In this chapter, I turn perhaps to the other end of the spectrum. Many investors believe that Treasuries, because of their low yields relative to historical levels, are one of the least attractive asset classes. Today, Treasuries may be the one asset about which you feel most averse. You might ask, "Why invest in an asset that offers a very low yield with potentially limited upside and significant downside risk?" It would be one thing if Treasuries were yielding double digits as they were in the 1980s, but yields near historic lows seem to make this an obviously poor asset class in which to invest. This mindset, while ostensibly reasonable, is flawed.

The conventional approach to assessing the attractiveness of asset classes, including Treasuries, is to consider the upside. The main question that is often asked is how much Treasuries can return over a reasonable time frame. Most investors look at the current yield as an indicator of the future return potential of Treasuries since the principal value is guaranteed. If interest rates are low relative to historical levels, then the assumption is that there is more downside risk than upside potential in Treasuries. This is because if rates are low, then they are more likely to rise than fall. Rising rates cause a loss in principal in Treasuries, while falling rates are a positive. This simplistic approach effectively covers the preponderance of the analysis done on this important asset class.

Treasuries, like equities, should be assessed through a balanced portfolio lens. They should be considered within the context of the total portfolio rather than as a stand-alone investment. Not only will this new insight help you to better understand the important role of Treasuries in a balanced portfolio, but you will also more clearly appreciate the flaws in conventional thinking when viewing Treasuries from this different vantage point.

WHAT ARE TREASURIES?

Treasury bonds are government-guaranteed instruments that promise to pay a fixed interest rate over time. The principal value of the bond has nearly zero risk of loss because the issuer, the US government, effectively has the ability to print money to repay the bondholder. As a result, Treasuries are widely considered to be risk-free. However, this is only true if you buy a bond and hold it to maturity. The price of Treasuries fluctuates every day because these bonds are publicly traded. The price moves as the future economic environment unfolds and as expectations of the future shift. Thus, you can lose money if the bond is sold prior to maturity. When I discuss Treasuries in this chapter and in this book, I am referring to bonds that are generally not held to maturity, because my emphasis is on trying to achieve stable returns through time *at the total portfolio level*. Thus, the volatility in the price of the bonds becomes an important (and valuable) consideration.

HOW DO TREASURIES PERFORM ACROSS DIFFERENT ENVIRONMENTS?

Treasuries, despite their low yield, still play an important role in well-balanced portfolios. In order to fully appreciate this conclusion, I will begin with the economic bias of Treasuries in terms of growth and inflation. You have already seen how these two factors influence equity prices, so a continuation of a similar thought process will now be applied to Treasuries.

Growth/Inflation Bias: Conceptual Framework

Weak growth benefits Treasuries because of the increasing likelihood of falling interest rates. This occurs because a weakening economic environment produces a reaction by the central bank to consider lowering interest rates to encourage borrowing to spur economic growth. When growth unexpectedly declines, it results in a move by the Fed that had not been anticipated by the market, because the falling growth itself had not been expected.

As a consequence, longer-term interest rates normally decline because cash rates suddenly are discounted to rise less than previously anticipated because of the surprisingly lower level of economic growth.

Lower interest rates benefit bond prices. More precisely, it is the future changes in cash rates that influences bond prices. This is because the bond yield at various maturities from short-term to long-term merely reflects the discounted changes in cash rates. Since the Fed controls cash rates and the Fed responds to changes in the economic environment (in terms of growth and inflation) by adjusting cash rates, then these economic shifts together impact discounted cash rates far into the future. Changes in cash rates then impact longer-term interest rates, which directly affect Treasury bond prices.

Declining interest rates are beneficial for Treasury prices because the bonds you own have a fixed interest rate. If prevailing rates are lower than those at the time of your purchase, then the higher coupon of your bond relative to market rates makes your bond a more attractive investment. Consequently, the price rises to reflect the new reality of lower interest rates.

Moreover, Treasuries tend to do well during weakening growth periods because of a flight to quality during adverse economic environments. When negative outcomes impact the economy, it seems reasonable that investors would react by becoming more cautious and risk averse. Treasuries, which have no credit risk, all of a sudden become more attractive investments because the focus shifts from maximizing returns to protecting capital. The high-quality bias of Treasuries attracts frightened investors who are seeking a safe place for their money.

Within this context you might better appreciate how it is possible for low interest rates to go even lower. All it takes is for economic growth to underperform what is already discounted. Since growth underperforms expectations roughly half the time from a historical standpoint, it makes sense that the next move in interest rates is roughly equally likely to be lower versus higher than current rates (even with low starting yields). The years 2019 and 2020 provided recent examples of low starting yields falling even lower despite repeated predictions for rising interest rates.

Lower inflation also benefits bond prices. As expressed earlier, the Fed attempts to keep inflation at bay by raising interest rates to deter borrowing when inflation is too high and lowering rates to stimulate debt growth when inflation is too low. Each incremental change in inflation produces an expectation of its future path. How that expectation relates to what has already been discounted in the original price is then reflected in the current price. If inflation falls more than expected, then that leads to a greater likelihood of the Fed lowering short-term interest rates in response. This new discovery then feeds into the increased probability of lower future long-term interest rates, which benefits Treasury prices.

In Chapter 3 on equities, I described the unique and challenging environment of deflation. The severe negative consequences of deflation – in contrast to the benefits of falling inflation – are precisely why central banks are so focused on avoiding this economic outcome. When inflation rates fall too low, there is great incentive for the Fed to lower interest rates to stimulate more borrowing in order to improve growth and increase the inflation rate. Central banks, generally speaking, prefer for inflation rates not to hover too close to zero for long. Keep in mind that deflation is historically quite rare, mainly because of the central bank's ability and willingness to avoid it at any cost. Further, the recent Japanese and European deflationary periods offer central banks vivid reminders of the severe social, political, and economic costs of such dire circumstances and the challenges of reversing these conditions.

This background about deflation relates to this section of the book because this particular economic environment should be examined on its own. It does not fit cleanly into the rising/falling growth and rising/falling inflation construct described earlier. Like the economic shock that comes from deflation, the impact of this environment on asset-class returns can also be drastic. Stock prices collapse an average of 90% and in most instances, deflation can lead to widespread bankruptcies and spikes in unemployment. Industrial commodities and inflation-linked bonds, both of which are pro-inflation investments, generally lose money as well. In fact, few asset classes hold their value as a mad rush into cash often dominates during these frightening periods. Treasury bonds may provide a safe haven, because their prices are most directly impacted by shifts in interest rates. Deflation is normally met by a drastic cut in short-term interest rates in an effort to promote borrowing and spending to curtail the deflationary spiral. Long-term rates also tend to fall precipitously as concerns about entrenched deflation mount. Japan offers an example of this dynamic, as their long-term government bonds fell from low levels to negative rates.

Therefore, Treasuries carry with them some unique deflation protection characteristics in addition to the falling inflation bias. Deflation does not occur frequently, so don't overvalue this characteristic. That said, if it does occur, you would be very glad that you own some long-term Treasuries. Think of it as insurance: you rarely need it, but it is prudent to keep it just in case. However, unlike insurance, which is generally expected to be a money-losing proposition (given that insurance companies tend to be profitable over time at the expense of policyholders), Treasuries have a positive expected return. Imagine if, rather than paying premiums to insure your home, the insurance company mailed you a check twice a year. Given the current state of the economy and the record debt levels that exist in most of the developed world, holding some deflation protection is prudent – particularly when you can purchase it with a positive expected return by investing in Treasuries.

Table 4.1 includes the addition of Treasuries to our tally of asset-class economic biases.

Table 4.1   Asset-Class Economic Biases

Economic Environment	Favored Asset Classes	
Rising Growth	Equities	
Falling Growth	Treasuries	
Rising Inflation		
Falling Inflation	Equities	Treasuries

Growth/Inflation Bias: Historical Returns

Figure 4.1 provides historical data that supports these cause–effect linkages. The rare deflationary periods that we've experienced have been bundled with falling inflation economic climates in this table (since both are good environments for Treasuries).

Figure 4.1   Annualized Long-Term Treasury Excess Returns by Economic Environment – January 1926 to March 2021

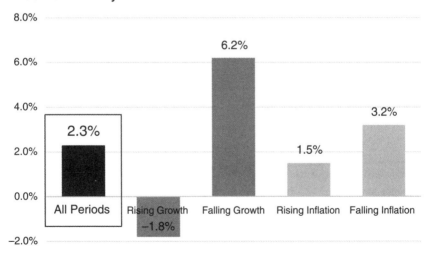

Source: Bloomberg. Methodology used to determine if growth and inflation are rising or falling: current growth or inflation rate compared to average of the trailing 12-month period. If the current rate (of growth/inflation) is higher, then that is considered a rising growth/inflation period and vice versa. The logic is based on the observation that most people expect the future to closely resemble the recent trend line.

As you might expect, at 2.3% the historical average excess return above cash is not as high as equities. Treasuries have the same credit risk as cash, so investors in long-term Treasuries only receive compensation for the interest rate risk that is taken. However, as is the case with equities, the difference in returns by economic environment is meaningful. During falling growth periods, the excess return of Treasuries has averaged 6.2% per year. This is a very strong average return that is comparable to the 5.3% equity average excess return (for all periods). Considering that about half the time growth is falling relative to expectations, it is easy to see the benefits of owning Treasuries as part of a balanced portfolio. Of course, the opposite environment of rising growth has historically been bad for Treasuries, with an average excess return of −1.8%. Predictably, Treasuries benefit from falling inflation and underperform during periods of rising inflation, as demonstrated in Figure 4.1.

The effective hedging benefits Treasuries offer relative to equities are worth highlighting. Because equities and Treasuries have the exact opposite economic bias to growth, their returns should diverge the most during severe growth shocks (both negative and positive). From a downside protection perspective, Table 4.2 summarizes the total returns of these two asset classes during the four largest equity bear markets of the millennium during which stocks fell at least 20% from peak to trough.

Table 4.2   Equities and Treasuries During Recent Bear Markets

Asset Class	2020 COVID-19 Pandemic (Jan 2020– Mar 2020)	2011 Eurozone Crisis (May 2011– Sep 2011)	2008 Credit Crisis (Nov 2007– Feb 2009)	2000 Dot-Com Crash (Apr 2000– Sep 2002)
Global Equities	−21%	−20%	−54%	−47%
Long-Term Treasuries	+21%	+26%	+17%	+35%

Source: Bloomberg.

I compare the returns of equities from peak to trough to Treasuries over the same period. While equities suffered a material loss of capital, Treasuries experienced a simultaneous bull market demonstrating the clear diversification benefits of including this asset class in a balanced allocation. Note that in each of these cases the starting yield of Treasuries was low before the downturn and fell even lower after the negative surprise. Table 4.3 lists the starting and ending yield for the same peak to trough periods.

Table 4.3   Starting and Ending 10-Year Treasury Yield During Recent Bear Markets

	2020 COVID-19 Pandemic (Jan 2020– Mar 2020)	2011 Eurozone Crisis (May 2011– Sep 2011)	2008 Credit Crisis (Nov 2007– Feb 2009)	2000 Dot-Com Crash (Apr 2000– Sep 2002)
Starting 10-Year Treasury Yield	1.92%	3.29%	4.47%	6.00%
Ending 10-Year Treasury Yield	0.67%	1.92%	3.01%	3.59%

Source: Bloomberg.

Investors were generally concerned about low rates before each of these unexpected downturns and, therefore, Treasuries were broadly underowned. Note that in early 2000, cash was yielding about the same as 10-year Treasuries, so the prevailing view at the time was that the 6% was unattractive even though it may sound high looking back. Additionally, the strong returns Treasuries earned repeatedly surprised market participants who were anticipating low returns because of the low starting yields. The point here isn't to suggest that Treasuries will have another 20% year soon. No one knows when the next negative growth surprise will occur or what will cause it. For instance, a global pandemic was an unforeseen catalyst prior to 2020. However, there can be much greater confidence in the benefits of diversification and the economic bias of Treasuries to rally in such an environment despite its cause (as we witnessed in the first quarter of 2020). In other words, the mechanics of what happens during a downturn are more predictable than the timing or cause of the negative event: economy unexpectedly weakens, the Fed cuts short-term interest rates in response, long-term interest rates fall in reaction to short-term rates dropping more than expected, Treasury prices appreciate.

The opposite also holds true. When growth surprises to the upside, Treasuries should be expected to underperform as interest rates rise. Table 4.4 lists the four strongest bull markets since 2000 and the corresponding equity and Treasury returns.

Table 4.4   Equities and Treasuries During Recent Bull Markets

Asset Class	Post-2020 COVID-19 Pandemic (Mar 2020– Mar 2021)	Post-2011 Eurozone Crisis (Sep 2011– Dec 2019)	Post-2008 Credit Crisis (Feb 2009– Apr 2011)	Post-2000 Dot-Com Crash (Sep 2002– Oct 2007)
Global Equities	54%	152%	94%	149%
Long-Term Treasuries	–16%	41%	6%	26%

Source: Bloomberg.

At a quick glance you may notice that a mix of equities and Treasuries is better off during a rising interest rate environment because equities rise more than Treasuries underperform their average (they have actually risen on average during these periods). During a weak period, the rise of Treasuries helps cushion the fall of equities. This is important because minimizing losses during economic downturns can materially improve long-term returns because of the asymmetry in the math: losses hurt so much more than gains help. If you lose 50%, then you need to earn 100% just to break even.

Treasuries and equities tend to work well together because of the opposite economic bias to growth. Note, however, that they both have the same bias to inflation (falling) so prudent diversification doesn't end there. This is the topic for the next two chapters as I cover the critical role of inflation hedges like TIPS, commodities, and gold in a well-balanced portfolio.

WHAT IS THE BEST WAY TO INVEST IN TREASURIES?

When investors think of Treasuries, safety and low risk immediately come to mind. This asset is often considered to be a safe haven where investors can park savings that they want to preserve. Most investors do not associate Treasuries with high returns.

It is important to understand that Treasuries may generally have low return and low risk, but their ratio of return to risk is comparable to that of equities. Therefore, if we increase the risk of Treasuries to the risk of stocks, we should be able to match the long-term return of stocks. Investors have two levers they can pull to raise the expected return (and risk) of Treasuries. Maturity is the primary lever, which any investor can access to increase return and risk of this asset class. Most investors buy shorter-maturity Treasuries (10 years or less) since they are seeking safety. However, investors can also buy longer-dated bonds as long as 30 years in maturity. These Treasuries are still guaranteed by the US government, so they are not riskier from a credit standpoint. Instead, the risk is purely interest rate risk. That is, as interest rates fall or rise (relative to expectations), longer-term Treasury prices move more than those of shorter-dated bonds. The term *duration* is a simple measure of the interest rate risk of a bond based on its future cash flows. The farther out the cash flows, the longer the duration, and the greater the bond price fluctuation when interest rates shift.

Long-maturity Treasuries are relatively risky investments from a price volatility standpoint. They can easily rise or fall 20% or more in a single year. However, owning longer-term Treasuries is still not enough risk/return to get us to equal the risk of equities. Thus, we need to pull the second lever by applying modest leverage. In other words, we need to own more of the long-term Treasuries than equities in order to get to an equal risk allocation. Another way to look at this is that we could compare the 100-year returns of long-term Treasuries to global equities, and we'd see that by adding a little bit of leverage we could have roughly equalized their returns and risk over a very long period of time looking backwards. We've all been taught that stocks outperform over the long run. How can a government-guaranteed bond provide the same expected return as risky equities? Long duration and a small amount of leverage are all it takes.

The only reason the returns in Figure 4.1 diverge materially between the good and bad periods is because we are using long-duration Treasuries. Shorter-duration Treasuries share exactly the same environmental bias as longer-term Treasuries. In fact, the excess returns above cash have been relatively close. However, the returns during good environments and bad environments would not be too different. Good periods would outperform the average excess return by a little bit, and bad environments would produce slight underperformance. This is simply because longer-duration bonds have more volatility than short-term bonds. More volatility means that the return pattern will fluctuate more, which leads to the wider divergence in returns during good and bad economic climates, resulting in higher highs and lower lows.

From a conventional perspective, when you have two asset classes that produce comparable long-term returns, you would always select the one that has less risk or lower volatility. Why take a lot more risk for a little more return? However, from a balanced portfolio viewpoint, you do not make asset allocation decisions based on the same criteria. Instead, the emphasis is on identifying the economic bias of each asset class and determining its volatility. As is apparent from Figure 4.1, the reason more volatility is preferred over less volatility (and therefore long-duration instead of short-duration Treasuries) is because of the better returns *when you need them*. This is the whole idea behind building balance. You focus less on each individual asset class and more on how it fits within the bigger picture. Each asset class is part of a team and serves a greater purpose. This can be a counterintuitive concept that will be repeated throughout this book.

Furthermore, when interest rates are very low, as they were when I wrote this book in 2021, longer-term Treasury rates have more room to fall than shorter-term bonds with lower yields. This is an important consideration, since the role of Treasuries is to rally during falling growth and falling inflation environments. Because there is effectively a floor at zero rates (or perhaps slightly negative as we've seen in other developed economies), Treasury price increases have a ceiling. The higher the interest rate, the higher the ceiling and the more protection Treasuries can offer. In a low-rate environment when longer-duration bonds have higher yields than shorter-duration, there is a strong balancing benefit that prevails from extending duration. Therefore, I use long-dated Treasuries for our risk parity portfolio.

We still need to determine the best vehicle to invest in this asset class with an eye towards low cost, low taxes, and high liquidity. As a reminder, we target low fees, high tax efficiency, and strong liquidity for our total risk parity portfolio, which requires a similar objective for each asset-class component.

One of the interesting aspects of Treasuries (unlike equities or commodities) is that there is little need for significant diversification. The only diversification decision relates to the maturity as opposed to the issuer (since there is only one). I opt to invest in the 10-year maturity and the 30-year maturity. By holding exposure to these points in the Treasury yield curve, we spread the risk of one part of the curve moving versus the other, while maintaining a long maturity profile overall. Later I explore the notion of potentially further diversifying this segment by investing in high-quality sovereign bonds of other countries. Here, I opt to keep the analysis simple by focusing solely on US Treasuries.

This approach makes investing in Treasuries relatively straightforward. As a result, there is little need to gain exposure through an exchange-traded fund (ETF) as suggested for equities. Since Treasuries are essentially risk free and all are supported by the same backstop, there's no clear advantage that comes from investing in a larger number of bonds. Therefore, I find no reason to pay an extra layer of fees that comes from a commingled vehicle when we can buy a few Treasuries for the desired allocation.

The typical way to own Treasuries is through physical bonds. However, a potentially more attractive option to gain exposure to Treasuries for larger investors is through the use of Treasury futures contracts, which are standardized contracts for the purchase and sale of US Treasuries for future delivery. The price of these contracts closely tracks the price of physical Treasury bonds. Moreover, the contracts are traded on an exchange, so they are extremely liquid investments and do not have counterparty risk.

These contracts require collateral and are settled every day to minimize the counterparty risk.

In terms of tax efficiency, Treasuries normally represent one of the least tax-efficient investments in our risk parity allocation. The yield of this asset class is treated as ordinary income, which is currently taxed at the highest federal rate. Treasury futures, however, come with better tax efficiency than physical Treasury bonds. This is because Treasury future returns are presently taxed at 60% long-term capital gains and 40% short-term capital gains rates. There are two advantages of this tax treatment over ordinary income rates. First, long-term capital gains rates are currently lower than ordinary income tax rates. Second, capital gains can be offset with capital losses, whereas income can be very difficult to offset within a portfolio context.

Another major advantage of using Treasury futures is that it allows for an inexpensive way to leverage the portfolio. Why do we need leverage? Going back to Figure 4.1, you will notice that the historical excess return of Treasuries over all environments has been lower than equities. A big part of the Risk Parity strategy is to structure each asset class to have comparable returns and risk so that there is no give-up in long-term returns by diversifying. Thus, we need to leverage long-term Treasuries to get them to similar expected returns as equities.

More specifically, equities have about 15% volatility historically, whereas long-term Treasuries have had about 11% volatility. To equalize the volatility, we would need to own about 40% more Treasuries than equities. This extra allocation is best achieved through the use of leverage as opposed to a reduction in the equity allocation. Using leverage allows the total portfolio to have a higher expected return. We will cover this step in greater detail in a later chapter.

ARE THERE EXTRAORDINARY ENVIRONMENTS TO CONSIDER?

Although the United States has never faced zero percent long-term interest rates, many other developed economies have. Japan has been saddled with zero rates for a few decades, and the eurozone has been trying to escape the same deflation trap for years. In fact, the trend of rates falling toward zero seems to have only intensified recently, particularly as the deflationary impact of the global pandemic has forced most interest rates across the globe to accelerate the downward trajectory.

Unlike all the other asset classes we've presented, Treasuries are unique in that there is a theoretical ceiling on its price. The value of Treasuries rises as interest rates fall (and vice versa). Rates can only drop to zero percent or possibly go a little negative, as we've seen in some countries. Since we can't count on negative rates, we can reasonably assume that prices can only rise until rates hit zero. This dynamic can introduce asymmetry in Treasury prospective returns: they can only go up so much but can drop without limit. Despite this premise seeming to be reasonable, investors and academics are debating it today. Bonds in Japan and several European countries with negative interest rates have continued to generate positive excess returns in recent years even after yields have fallen below zero.

From a balanced portfolio perspective, the question we are always asking ourselves is if economic growth surprises to the downside, which asset is likely to perform well? A secondary, and yet critical, question is whether the asset price can increase enough to provide sufficient balance from underperformance in other asset classes that are biased to do poorly during the same environment? The tendency of Treasuries to go up during an economic downturn is well established. However, from a mechanical standpoint, if long-term interest rates get close enough to zero, then Treasuries may not rise enough to properly balance the portfolio. For instance, if the 30-year Treasury yield is 0.25% and drops to 0%, then Treasuries wouldn't appreciate as much as if the rate fell from 1% to 0%.

We can use the bond's duration to measure the potential upside of Treasuries at various interest rate levels. Recall that duration is a measure of the interest rate risk of a bond. The longer the duration, the greater the interest-rate risk. Duration typically coincides with the bond's maturity, although they are different figures from one another. The general rule of thumb is the price of the bond will rise by the duration for every 1% decline in interest rates and vice versa. For example, if the duration is 20 years, then an investor in that Treasury bond will see 20% price appreciation if rates drop by 1%. The total return will be about 20% plus the interest paid on the bond. Conversely, if interest rates rise by 1%, then the investor loses about 20% minus the interest earned (which is paid as income). If rates move by 0.5%, then the price change is about half of 20%, or 10% in this case.

Going back to our previous example as a point of reference, if a 30-year bond has a 0.25% coupon and yield, then the rough duration is about 28 years. Therefore, if the market yield drops to 0%, then the Treasury would appreciate approximately 7%. If rates declined from 1% to 0%, then the price would increase about 26% (since the duration at a 1% coupon and yield would be about 26 years).

Should interest rates drop to very low levels, then Treasuries may not offer the required upside during weak economic environments. This would require adding other asset classes in place of or as a complement to Treasuries. Some assets to consider include non-US bonds that offer higher yields with comparable safety. These bonds would also serve to further diversify the nominal bond allocation. Perhaps more gold would work since the odds of quantitatively easing during the next downturn increase if rates are pinned at zero. Another consideration is US government agency bonds such as Government National Mortgage Association (commonly known as Ginnie Maes), which is high-quality mortgage debt issued by a government-owned corporation of the United States. Again, the core question is what would likely do well if the economy were to unexpectedly weaken.

SUMMARY

Of all the potential economic environments that you would likely want to cover in your portfolio, it is the falling growth scenario that is perhaps the most significant. The worst equity bear markets in history occurred during the weakest economic environments, and more accurately, during the periods in which most investors had expected continued good times but were suddenly blindsided by unexpected downturns (i.e., Q1 2020, 2008–2009, 2000–2002, 1973–1974, 1929–1932, etc.).

With this understanding, the recent moves by investors to cut exposure to Treasuries in favor of lower-quality, higher-yielding bonds and to drastically reduce duration can be re-examined. It may be more apparent now why these actions have actually increased the risk in the portfolio by making the allocation less diversified. Many investors are concerned about the risk of rising interest rates. Yes, there is risk of loss in Treasuries if interest rates rise (as they did in 2013 and in early 2021), but there is also risk of loss in the rest of the portfolio if interest rates fall (usually because of a weakening economic environment). This became apparent in 2008 and first quarter 2020. The most important message to remember is that it is far better to hedge the interest rate risk by adding asset classes that are biased to do well during environments in which rates rise than it is to significantly reduce Treasury exposure.

An important reminder is that economic growth has historically underperformed about half the time. This observation has been true since 1926 and is likely to persist looking forward. This is a reasonable outcome, because what really matters is how future economic conditions play out versus what has already been discounted. The consensus view about future growth is factored into today's price of Treasuries (as well as equities, commodities, TIPS, and all other asset classes).

It makes sense that the consensus, or average, view is wrong about half the time for two main reasons. First, the middle point of a data set means that half the outcomes fall below and half above that point. Second, the consensus view generally represents an extrapolation of the recent past into the near future. Most people expect the next 6 to 12 months to resemble the past 6 to 12 months. Few try to anticipate inflection points, and even fewer foresee major shifts before the fact.

The same can be said about inflation. Roughly half the time, what transpires is above what had been discounted, and the other half is below. Importantly, this range of outcomes exists whether interest rates are high or low. Everyone can easily observe the level of current interest rates and therefore factors this into expectations of future growth and inflation.

This background is repeated here because it is fundamental to describing the important role of Treasuries in the balanced portfolio. The same background is also crucial for establishing the importance of each asset class within the context of a truly balanced asset allocation.

One core idea behind the concept of maintaining a well-balanced portfolio is that you do not have to correctly guess which way interest rates are going to go. If rates move against you, then other parts of the portfolio are biased to outperform during that environment. If rates move favorably for Treasuries, then that is likely because of an adverse economic environment that would simultaneously cause other parts of the balanced portfolio to underperform. Therefore, if you don't maintain sufficient duration, then you leave the portfolio exposed to environments during which Treasuries are biased to outperform. If the economy suddenly weakens and you don't have enough duration in your Treasuries, then this part of the portfolio would not go up enough to offset underperformance elsewhere.

Each asset class in the balanced portfolio fills a specific role because it serves to cover certain economic environments. If one of the asset classes were removed from the efficient starting point, then the portfolio would naturally be exposed to the economic environment that had been previously covered by that asset class. Going back to our engine example, if you take out a piece of the engine because it doesn't seem like it's doing anything at the moment, you risk an engine that will malfunction in the future.

The two economic environments that Treasuries cover are weak growth and falling inflation (or deflation). Weak growth is the more important of the two, since most portfolios are already underweight weak-growth assets (either because of a lower quality bias in bonds, smaller total allocation to Treasuries, or a shorter duration). In other words, if long-term Treasuries are reduced from the neutral mix, then there is effectively a big bet that the economy will outperform expectations. Remember that economic growth disappoints expectations about half the time, because it is relative to market-discounted conditions. If you underweight Treasuries and the economy does weaken, then overall portfolio underperformance is likely to result because of the imbalance in the portfolio due to the underweight to Treasuries.

Putting it all together, it should be understandable why a core allocation to long-term Treasuries should have a permanent place in your balanced portfolio. Furthermore, the low yield should not deter you from owning this asset class because of the critical role it plays within the foundation of a well-balanced mix of asset classes.

CHAPTER FIVE

TIPS

In the previous two chapters I introduced equities and Treasuries through a balanced portfolio framework. I also showed how equities and Treasuries tend to complement each other well when considered within the context of a balanced portfolio. Equities are biased to outperform when economic growth is improving, and Treasuries generally do well in the opposite environment of weak growth. The reason you can't end there and construct a balanced portfolio using just these two asset classes is because there are two key economic inputs into asset-class price fluctuations. Stocks and Treasuries successfully cover you for different growth outcomes, but what about unexpected shifts in inflation? Both equities and Treasuries are biased to underperform during rising inflation (and outperform during falling inflation). In order to adequately build a well-balanced portfolio that covers all major environments, it's crucial to include additional asset classes in your portfolio that are biased to outperform during rising inflationary climates. In this chapter, I discuss the benefits of incorporating Treasury Inflation-Protected Securities (TIPS) into a balanced portfolio. TIPS are the first of two major asset classes offering inflation protection that will be analyzed (commodities will be covered in the next chapter).

Most investors do not fully appreciate the benefits of TIPS. In fact, this asset class is entirely missing in most conventional portfolios. In this chapter, I first clarify what TIPS are and how they work. Similar to Treasuries, many investors are opposed to adding TIPS as part of their portfolio simply because the yield is low relative to historical levels. The flaws in this conventional perspective will become apparent as I explain the crucial role TIPS play within the context of a balanced portfolio and why this unique asset class is difficult to replace.

WHAT ARE TIPS?

TIPS are bonds issued by the US government. Accordingly, they carry the same credit risk as Treasury bonds, which were addressed in the last chapter. That is to say that TIPS, like Treasuries, are widely considered to be a risk-free asset, since the US government holds the world's reserve currency and has the capability to print US dollars to repay its obligations.

TIPS generally pay a coupon that is less than that paid by Treasuries. This is because TIPS holders receive the coupon plus actual inflation (measured by using the CPI, or the consumer price index), which accrues to the principal over time. For example, if you buy a TIPS bond that provides a 1% yield to maturity, your total return will be 1% plus actual inflation if you hold the bond to maturity. If inflation turns out to be 3%, then you get 4% (1% plus 3%). The main idea behind a TIPS bond is to provide investors the inflation protection that they do not receive with Treasuries. Other than the inflation component, TIPS and Treasuries are the same. Of course, that inflation factor makes a world of difference (as you may have guessed).

Another way to compare Treasuries to TIPS is by calculating the break-even inflation rate. For instance, if a 10-year Treasury offers a yield of 4% and a comparable maturity TIPS bond has a yield of 1%, then that implies that the market is discounting inflation to be 3% over the maturity time frame. This must be true because the two bonds are identical otherwise (same maturity and credit quality). The only difference between the two is that one provides a yield without inflation protection and the other offers a lower yield with inflation protection. As an investor, you have an opportunity to choose between the two securities. Therefore, if you feel that inflation will be greater than the break-even rate – 3% in this example – then you would opt for the TIPS bond. If you were concerned that inflation would come in less than 3%, then you'd buy the Treasury because it would provide a higher total return if you are correct.

You might sensibly consider TIPS to be one of the safest investments you can make: They are bonds, and therefore your principal is safely returned to you in real terms at a predetermined maturity date. Your investment is guaranteed by the US government and is backed by its ability and willingness to print money to pay you back. For lending your money, you are paid a fixed interest rate that is also guaranteed. Furthermore, and perhaps most important, your investment is protected against the long-term negative consequences of inflation. Other bond investments do not share this benefit. Treasuries, for instance, are just as safe in terms of principal and interest payments, but because they are not linked to inflation you are taking the risk that the money paid back to you will be worth less due to inflation. Thus, TIPS are arguably safer than Treasuries, since an investment in this asset class does not contain inflation risk as an investment in Treasuries does.

For example, if you lend me $100 today and I promise to pay you back in 10 years, then the expected rate of inflation is a big factor in the amount of interest you would charge me for that loan. If you anticipate inflation to be low, then less interest is required. However, if you suspect that inflation rates will spike, then you will demand a higher rate of interest in order to be compensated for the diminished purchasing power of your money over time. With TIPS, this concern is generally eliminated.

Interestingly, TIPS are not widely followed securities, and many investors misunderstand them relative to Treasuries and other nominal (as opposed to inflation-linked) bonds. This is partly understandable because TIPS are relatively new securities. In the United States, they were first created in 1997, whereas other parts of the world initiated similar instruments a decade or two earlier. Although 20-plus years may sound like a long time, that pales in comparison to most other asset classes like stocks and nominal bonds that have been around for over 100 years. The confusion is probably due partially to this asset class's relative young life and partially because of its distinctive structure. It simply does not function like most other bonds because it is hedged against inflation (one of the greatest enemies of a bond holder).

Taxable investors should be aware of the unique tax treatment of TIPS. The annual CPI adjustment is taxed as if the income was distributed to investors even though it was not. This "phantom income" can result in a greater tax liability than would be typical for the level of actual income received. This can make TIPS one of the least tax-efficient investments in the risk parity portfolio.

HOW DO TIPS PERFORM ACROSS DIFFERENT ENVIRONMENTS?

The two key insights about each asset class on which I focused when discussing equities and Treasuries will be repeated with TIPS. The economic environments during which TIPS are biased to outperform will be explored and the logical connections analyzed. Since limited actual history is available for TIPS the reasonableness of the cause–effect relationships is even more significant than it is with other asset classes.

Growth/Inflation Bias: Conceptual Framework

TIPS are fixed-income securities that are biased to outperform during periods of rising inflation. The rising inflation benefit is more obvious with TIPS than with just about any other asset class. Returns to TIPS owners are adjusted by the actual rate of inflation. Therefore, the higher the rate of inflation, the greater the amount received. In many ways TIPS are arguably the purest inflation hedge available to investors. There is a direct pass-through benefit from rising inflation to TIPS investors.

Note that TIPS, in this sense, have the opposite environmental bias to inflation than Treasuries, which do better during falling inflationary periods. This makes sense since TIPS returns are inflation-adjusted, whereas those from Treasuries are not. With Treasuries, you are betting that inflation won't be higher than discounted, because if it is, then the fixed interest rate that the Treasury pays you would be too low. With a TIPS bond you don't have to worry about the inflation rate since you will automatically receive it.

TIPS move on changes in real interest rates (which are nominal rates minus inflation). By taking the nominal yield curve and subtracting expected inflation at each maturity date, you get the real yield curve. How real rates change through time versus discounted levels is what ultimately influences TIPS prices and performance. Unexpected shifts in economic growth and inflation have a direct impact on real interest rates and therefore TIPS prices are heavily influenced by this factor.

The inflation component of TIPS is the key attribute that makes this asset class particularly attractive. There are few inflation hedges available to investors, and none of the other options offers as clean a hedge as TIPS, particularly over the long term. We have not experienced high inflation since the 1970s and early 1980s, so you may be wondering why you need inflation protection. Keep in mind that inflation does not have to be high for inflation hedges to outperform. Recall that with all asset classes, the pricing is impacted by how the future transpires relative to what was discounted. If inflation expectations are low, then all it takes is a little more inflation for TIPS to be positively impacted. This is especially true when no one is expecting high inflation (perhaps because it has not occurred for several decades) and such an outcome transpires. Many asset classes would likely underperform in this scenario. This potential outcome is certainly possible in the current economic environment because what happens will be largely dependent on how much money the Fed eventually creates. If the amount of quantitative easing is large enough such that total spending increases materially, then high inflation is certainly a possibility. In short, it would be a mistake to assume that the relative stability of contained inflation over the past few decades is likely to continue indefinitely, particularly given present unusual and uncertain economic circumstances.

Falling growth periods are also positive for TIPS because of the prospect of falling interest rates in response to weakening economic conditions. The fixed real-interest-rate component of TIPS results in a positive influence on the price, as downward pressure on competing interest rates materializes. Note that, if inflation declines more than discounted during these periods, TIPS would be negatively impacted. Thus, it is the net effect of nominal (or normal) interest rates and inflation shifts that ultimately move TIPS prices.

Every component of the balanced portfolio serves a critical role. TIPS, however, are possibly the most diversifying of the asset classes. As I have discussed throughout this book, your objective in portfolio construction should be to ensure that you have efficiently covered all four key economic environments (rising growth, falling growth, rising inflation, and falling inflation) with the asset classes you have selected. As it turns out, some of the boxes are easier to fill than others. There are many asset classes that are biased to do well during rising growth environments. Falling inflation is also easy to cover since both stocks and bonds, which are widely used, benefit from this outcome. There are a handful of asset classes that are predisposed to outperform during falling growth periods, but after that the list starts to shrink. As previously mentioned, even fewer benefit from rising inflation. In fact, the list of good candidates for this environment is quite limited. Therefore, due to the scarcity of viable replacements to cover the rising inflation and falling growth outcomes, TIPS serve as an excellent diversifier for most portfolios.

Since the growth and inflation boxes for TIPS are exactly the opposite from those used for equities, you might conclude that a balanced portfolio can be constructed by using just these two asset classes. After all, between the two, all four potential economic outcomes would be covered. Indeed, this is a valid argument, and a portfolio that only consists of these two assets would probably be more balanced than conventional portfolios.

However, one unique nuance about the timing of TIPS returns should be mentioned. Since TIPS returns are adjusted for actual inflation, it is generally shifts in actual inflation that impact TIPS returns rather than shifts in expected inflation (or how future inflation transpires relative to expectations). This distinction is significant in terms of the exact timing of the underperformance and outperformance of TIPS. Because of the fact that TIPS are bonds that account for the current inflation rate, over the short term their price is typically not materially impacted by shifts in future expectations of inflation changes. However, over longer time periods, the changes in inflation do make a difference in the returns of TIPS, because investors receive returns reflecting the inflation that actually transpires. This characteristic is only important because of the potential timing mismatch between TIPS returns and those of the other asset classes. Because the returns of the other asset classes mentioned – equities, Treasuries, and commodities – are impacted by changes in inflation expectations and how inflation transpires relative to what had been expected, the key impact to the returns of these asset classes is how these variables shift over time. Consequently, TIPS may not move if inflation expectations suddenly increase (unless real yields simultaneously fall), as would the other asset classes. Of course, over time TIPS do react to these changes, but the shift in returns experiences a lag relative to the other asset classes.

Think of it this way: TIPS prices over the short run are based on changes in growth, whereas shifts in inflation flow through TIPS over a longer time frame. In contrast, the other three asset classes experience changes in the current price from shifts in growth as well as inflation over the short run (as well as the long run). The upshot is if inflation expectations suddenly jump, then the lag in TIPS returns reacting to this new environment may not immediately be reflected in the price. This means that the balanced portfolio may underperform for a short time until TIPS returns catch up to the change in conditions. They need to catch up because the other three asset classes would have already reacted to the shift in inflation expectations while TIPS experienced a delayed reaction. Over time, this distinction is smoothed out so it is not that important over the long run. I only mention it so that you are aware of this unique dynamic as it relates to TIPS. One way to mitigate this factor is to also own commodities (which will be covered in detail in Chapter 6) as an inflation hedge, because this asset class does tend to react immediately to shifts in inflation expectations (in large part because increases in commodity prices actually cause inflation, since commodities are the raw inputs to the consumer goods the prices of which CPI measures). For this reason, there is a benefit to further diversifying a balanced portfolio by adding more assets within the framework presented.

Additionally, given the unusual state of the current environment, there are several courses through which rising inflation may surface looking forward. During the 1970s, inflation rose because of rising wages and commodity prices, particularly from the oil shocks of 1973 and 1979. In the United States, wages have not materially risen for over a decade and until recently little pressure has been building in this area, and commodity prices have been relatively weak as well. However, there have been trillions of dollars of quantitative easing over the same time frame that could ultimately result in monetary inflation. That is, excessive minting of new fiat currency may be the next cause of broad inflation as the supply of money outpaces the supply of goods and services. In addition, the commodities supply may shrink given the lack of capital expenditures to expand production in recent years. And labor supply may also dwindle as more of the population ages out of the workforce. Both potential developments would put upward pressure on prices. As a result, a more diverse set of inflation hedges that are biased to outperform during various forms of inflation may be prudent.

Table 5.1 inserts TIPS into our favored asset class by economic environment table.

Table 5.1   Asset-Class Economic Biases

Economic Environment	Favored Asset Classes	
Rising Growth	Equities	
Falling Growth	Treasuries	TIPS
Rising Inflation	TIPS	
Falling Inflation	Equities	Treasuries

Growth/Inflation Bias: Historical Returns

TIPS are biased to outperform their average excess return above cash during rising inflation and falling growth economic climates. Figure 5.1 summarizes the data that supports the conceptual conclusions covered earlier.

Figure 5.1   Annualized Long-Term TIPS Excess Returns by Economic Environment – April 1998 to March 2021

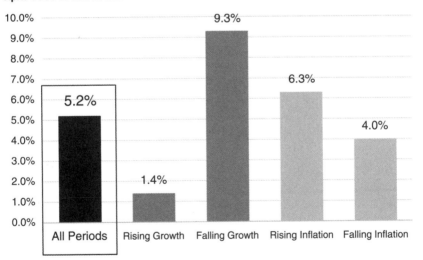

Source: Bloomberg. Methodology used to determine if growth and inflation are rising or falling: current growth or inflation rate compared to average of the trailing 12-month period. If the current rate (of growth/inflation) is higher, then that is considered a rising growth/ inflation period and vice versa. The logic is based on the observation that most people expect the future to closely resemble the recent trend line.

As can be expected, TIPS outperformed their average returns during rising inflationary periods. Falling growth environments also produced very strong returns. Unsurprisingly, the opposite environments – namely, rising growth and falling inflation – delivered below-average results. Note that because a material inflationary period has not unfolded since 1998, the data may understate the true impact of major shifts in inflation on relative returns.

WHAT IS THE BEST WAY TO INVEST IN TIPS?

For exactly the same reasons that I proposed the use of long-term Treasuries rather than shorter-term bonds, longer-duration TIPS are appropriate within the context of a balanced portfolio. It is probably even more critical to include longer-term TIPS than long-term Treasuries in a balanced portfolio because of the unique economic bias of TIPS. Rising inflation and falling growth is exactly the opposite economic bias of equities. Since most conventional portfolios own a high allocation to equities, TIPS turn out to be the perfect diversifier and should be included in nearly every portfolio. Additionally, a more volatile version of TIPS is prudent in order to provide sufficient exposure to the underexposed economic biases covered by TIPS.

As with Treasuries, you should not be overly concerned about rising interest rates negatively impacting the returns of the long-duration TIPS in your portfolio. The economic climate that tends to be the worst for TIPS is the best for equities. Thus, if TIPS perform poorly, it is most likely because of unexpected shifts in the economic environment that would concurrently produce outperformance in the most commonly held asset in portfolios: equities. We saw this play out in 2013 as TIPS suffered big losses as growth outperformed expectations and inflation fell. Of course, equities performed exceptionally well during the same environment, as you should expect. Ultimately, the reason to own longer-duration TIPS is to properly hedge against environments of falling growth, rising inflation, or both, so that you will have sufficient upside to cover for weakness elsewhere in the portfolio.

Similar to Treasuries, TIPS also do not require broad diversification. All TIPS are issued by the US government and are guaranteed by its full faith and credit. Therefore, we do not need to own many TIPS bonds to achieve sufficient diversification. As with Treasuries, we only need to be concerned with the maturity of the bonds that we purchase. Since our focus is on longer-term bonds, the universe of options is fairly limited. I suggest bonds with maturities of 10+ years comparable to the Treasury holdings.

Since buying a few bonds provides the needed diversification, there is also little need to gain exposure through a mutual fund or ETF. By directly investing in the physical TIPS bonds, we can avoid an added layer of fees that come with fund investments. As of this writing, TIPS futures are not available, so the approach of gaining exposure using a similar investment vehicle as Treasuries is currently not an option.

It should be noted that other countries also offer inflation-linked bonds, and, in fact, this market began outside of the United States, with regions like the UK having a much longer history than US TIPS. Diversifying across countries is fine, but I currently opt to maintain only US inflation-linked bonds to minimize the currency risk and taxes associated with foreign bonds. Many of these markets are generally less liquid than the US market as well.

ARE THERE EXTRAORDINARY ENVIRONMENTS TO CONSIDER?

TIPS are generally biased to outperform during environments of rising inflation and falling growth. However, periods characterized by deflation (inflation falling below zero) pose special risks for TIPS. Sometimes weakening growth can occur during a deflationary period (like in the 1930s or September/October 2008). This outcome can transpire when the economy collapses driving consumer prices to similarly fall, resulting in deflation. In environments of weakening growth that is also deflationary, TIPS can fail to outperform and provide the needed downside growth protection that is inherent in typical falling growth periods not associated with deflation.

There are two protections against a deflationary period that investors can utilize. First, TIPS bonds pay holders actual inflation with a floor at zero. That is, if inflation goes negative (i.e., deflation), then the bonds do not charge investors the negative inflation prints. However, this only applies to newly issued TIPS bonds. After a TIPS bond comes to market, the principal value increases by inflation every year and pays out the cumulative gain once the bond matures. Investors who sell the bond before maturity still benefit from the accrued inflation, because the purchaser of the bond essentially pays the seller the current market value of the TIPS bond, which includes the accrued inflation premiums. Therefore, TIPS that are more seasoned would have less deflation protection than those that are newly issued with no accrued inflation appreciation. For example, if you bought a TIPS bond that just came out and we go through a deflationary period, then the principal value of the TIPS would not fall below par. However, if instead you were to own a TIPS that was issued 10 years ago (even with the same maturity date as the newly issued bond) and that bond had accrued 20% of inflation appreciation over the past 10 years (from let's say 2% per year of realized inflation), then you would suffer losses during the deflationary environment. If deflation was −2%, then your 20% of embedded appreciation would fall to 18%, whereas a newly issued TIPS would stay flat. Since you bought the bond with 20% of appreciation built in, then you actually lose 2% even though the bond price doesn't fall below par.

The second way for a TIPS holder to potentially protect against a deflationary climate is to replace TIPS with other assets that may *appreciate* during such an environment. After all, this is the idea of a well-balanced portfolio: own assets that are sensitive to varying economic drivers so that some go up while others may underperform. Shifting to newly issued TIPS would only reduce declines from principal value during deflation, as opposed to rising during an environment when many other assets are biased to precipitously fall, as is common during deflation.

One option is to use a mix of Treasuries and gold as a substitute for TIPS during a deflationary period. For this analysis we should revert to the core objective of holding TIPS in the first place. TIPS are designed to outperform during periods characterized by rising inflation and falling growth (in all but deflationary environments). As described in Chapter 4, Treasuries are a falling-growth asset, even during deflation. In fact, Treasuries may be one of the best assets to own when deflation occurs. Gold, on the other hand, is more of an inflation hedge (as will be fully explained in Chapter 6). Gold can also serve as a deflation hedge because of the increased likelihood of quantitative easing to reverse the downturn and the potential flight to a valuable storehold of wealth when there's a crisis of confidence in the system. Think of what would happen if we slipped into deflation. The economy has crumbled, and prices are falling the way they were during the Great Depression or in the depths of the Great Financial Crisis of 2008–2009. Policy makers would probably react by cutting interest rates (which benefits Treasuries) and initiating quantitative easing (which is good for gold). These are the likely measures that would be needed to engineer an economic recovery. Together, Treasuries and gold can provide similar economic exposure as TIPS, but with improved deflation protection.

Making this swap should not be viewed as a tactical move, which would be in contrast to the static, timeless approach held in this book. The idea is to maintain strong balance at all times to minimize the need to predict which economic environment will transpire next. We should always ask the question, "Which asset is biased to outperform if growth disappoints or if inflation falls or if there's deflation," and so on. TIPS do the job if growth disappoints except during deflationary environments.

Thus, when the deflation alarms are sounding, then balance may look slightly different from all other periods because TIPS don't offer the same downside growth protection. Thus, when the risk of deflation is heightened, then the shift described earlier makes sense. This doesn't mean that the entire TIPS position has to be replaced with Treasuries and gold. A portion would likely suffice, particularly since the environment could shift once again without much notice.

There is one other important difference between TIPS and Treasuries worth mentioning. In the previous chapter we described the challenges Treasuries may face, as interest rates get close to 0%, which limits the appreciation potential of these bonds. Reduced upside introduces asymmetry wherein investors potentially have more to lose than gain. Interest rates have a theoretical floor while there is no ceiling.

TIPS do not face the same limits. This is because TIPS price off of the real yield curve in contrast to the nominal yield curve that governs Treasuries. Nominal yields typically have a zero bound limit whereas real yields can go significantly negative. Recall that real yields are merely nominal yields minus expected inflation rates. If expected inflation rises and nominal yields stay low, then real yields can venture into negative territory. Consider that the historical low in the 10-year Treasury yield of around 0.3% was recently reached in March 2020 amid the COVID-19 pandemic. Prior to the recent drop in rates, the 10-year had never fallen below 1% in recorded history. On the other hand, 10-year *real* yields were negative at certain points in the 1920s, 1940s, 1950s and during the past two decades of the 2010s and 2020s.[1] In early 2020, the 10-year real interest rate dropped to –1%. During the 1940s it fell to around –5%, and it hit near –10% in the 1920s.[2] As a result of the potential for real yields to go far below 0%, TIPS have much greater appreciation potential during periods of low interest rates than Treasuries.

SUMMARY

In my experience, most portfolios are underweight inflation hedges. This may make sense since we have not experienced high inflation in the United States since the 1970s. However, central banks are intent on creating inflation to keep economies out of the spiral of deflation and have the power of the printing presses to help accomplish their objective. They may also likely allow inflation to rise as they did in the 1970s as the trade-off between growth and inflation becomes more acute (i.e., if the

[1]https://www.treasury.gov/resource-center/data-chart-center/interest-rates/Pages/TextView. aspx?data=realyieldAll
[2]Deutsche Bank.

alternative of tamping down on inflation would have a severe, intolerable impact on growth). TIPS represent the purest inflation hedge as a government guaranteed instrument that pays actual inflation to its investors. Additionally, from a balanced portfolio perspective, TIPS are an excellent diversifier that cannot easily be replaced. Their role within the context of a well-balanced portfolio is crucial because they cover the two economic scenarios that are most often underweighted – namely, falling growth and rising inflation.

CHAPTER SIX

Commodities

Assets that are biased to perform better during environments of rising inflation are generally more difficult to find than traditional investments. As described in previous chapters, the most commonly held asset classes – stocks and nominal bonds – both tend to outperform during falling inflation periods and underperform during the opposite environment. To better balance portfolios, inflation hedge assets are needed, particularly given recent indications by major central banks to target higher rates of inflation as levels have trended down for many years.

In Chapter 5 I explained how TIPS provide reliable inflation protection and perhaps serve as the purest hedge to rising consumer prices. Commodities are also effective inflation hedges that should be included in any well-balanced asset allocation. In fact, commodity prices are usually a major component of the actual inflation measure.

WHAT ARE COMMODITIES?

There are two broad categories of commodities: natural resources extracted from the earth and agricultural products or livestock. Natural resources include industrial metals (copper, aluminum, zinc, nickel), precious metals (gold, silver), energy (crude oil, natural gas), water, and timber. Agricultural/livestock includes commodities such as corn, sugar, soybeans, coffee, cattle, and hogs.

The prices of these commodities fluctuate based on shifting demand and supply. Changes in demand come from the economic cycles that we are trying to diversify against. For example, corn provides food for humans, but is also the main ingredient in livestock feed and an ingredient for ethanol production. If there was a sudden surge in corn demand for either of these purposes, then the price would likely rise since it takes several months to plant, grow, and harvest corn, causing the supply increase to lag growing demand. Other commodities work the same way.

HOW DO COMMODITIES PERFORM ACROSS DIFFERENT ENVIRONMENTS?

As we have gone through the first three asset classes – equities, Treasuries, and TIPS – you may have noticed that each has a different bias to growth and inflation changes. Equities do better when growth is rising and inflation falling. TIPS have the opposite bias of falling growth and rising inflation. Treasuries cover falling growth and falling inflation. Putting it together, we have two checks for assets biased to outperform during falling inflation (stocks and Treasuries), one for rising inflation (TIPS), two for falling growth (Treasuries and TIPS) and one for rising growth (stocks). This is summarized in Table 6.1.

Table 6.1   Asset-Class Economic Biases

Economic Environment	Favored Asset Classes	
Rising Growth	Equities	
Falling Growth	Treasuries	TIPS
Rising Inflation	TIPS	
Falling Inflation	Equities	Treasuries

The asset class of commodities helps round out our balanced mix because of its unique bias to outperform during rising inflation and rising growth, the two market environments in which we only have one asset class to this point. Since the ultimate goal of a balanced portfolio is to be indifferent to the economic environment, it is critical that we diversify across assets biased to do well in different climates *and* ensure that there is roughly equal exposure to each growth and inflation environment. Thus, it is important to think in these terms when selecting asset classes and why it is helpful to have commodities included in our risk parity portfolio.

Growth/Inflation Bias: Conceptual Framework

Commodities are biased to outperform during periods characterized by rising inflation. This bias is reasonable since rising prices in commodities such as energy, metals, and food directly and indirectly lead to broader increases in inflation measurements. The direct impacts on inflation figures come from the fact that the methodology used to calculate the CPI index incorporates changes in the prices of commodities. Meanwhile, indirect effects of rising commodity prices find their way into inflation of other items in the CPI basket because of the fact that these commodities are inputs into the prices of these items. For instance, higher oil prices result in increased gas prices that lead to higher prices for traveling or shipping items because of the boosted costs to those companies providing these services. At least a portion of the higher input expenses are typically passed on to consumers via higher prices, which results in higher overall prices for goods and services (and hence inflation).

The fact that commodities represent a portion of the input cost of goods and services is another reason there is an inflation link in their returns. As general increased demand for goods and services pushes overall inflation rates higher, the higher demand for the goods and services leads to greater demand for the inputs (the commodities). The higher demand in turn exerts upward pressure on commodity prices. If the demand was greater than expected, then the price generally rises, since the demand originally expected was based on the original supply in the prevailing market price.

Commodities are not only pro-inflation assets but also biased to outperform during rising growth environments. As the economy outperforms to the upside, greater commodity demand naturally follows. If you earn more money, then you are likely to spend a portion of that higher income. Part of that spending will either be directly on commodities (perhaps higher-quality food, oil, or precious metals) or on other goods and services that will require more commodities to produce. Since economic growth is greater than expected in this scenario, it is reasonable that the original supply of commodities is insufficient to meet the higher, newly generated demand. This mismatch generally results in upward price pressures, as demand outstrips supply. Imagine if there was great optimism about the future prospects of the economy: We are living in a boom period and this prosperity is expected to continue. This view would likely result in higher prices for commodities, as well as an uptick in the production of commodities. If you are a commodities producer and observe the economy is trending positively and commodity prices are rising, you will have the incentive to produce more commodities to meet the anticipated growing demand. Such lofty expectations are often not met, because the margin of safety has shrunk. Even if the economy performs well, it would have to do better than expected in order to positively impact commodities prices (or stock prices, or the price of any pro-growth asset class). Note that commodities could still potentially do well with stable but strong growth if there is a shortage of supply. Thus, in the case of commodities, changes in both supply and demand lead to price changes, and both are directly impacted by expectations of future economic conditions.

We have now completed our asset-class economic bias matrix as displayed in Table 6.2.

Table 6.2   Asset-Class Economic Biases

Economic Environment	Favored Asset Classes	
Rising Growth	Equities	Commodities
Falling Growth	Treasuries	TIPS
Rising Inflation	TIPS	Commodities
Falling Inflation	Equities	Treasuries

Commodity Futures versus Commodity Equities

Commodities are different from stocks, Treasuries, or TIPS in that they are not financial assets. Rather, commodities are real assets that can be physically touched. Of course, purchasing and storing crude oil or cattle is impractical for most investors. There are two general ways to invest in commodities without having to deal with the administrative burden and cost of holding the physical asset. First, you can enter into a futures contract with another party for the price of the various commodities. This approach to buying commodities provides a tight correlation with the underlying commodity price since you are essentially betting on price changes. The way these agreements work is you invest in a contract with another party in which you promise to pay a fixed price at a future date for a specific commodity. This price, called the futures price, may be higher or lower than the current price of that commodity, termed the spot price. For example, if the spot price of oil is $50 per barrel today, the price you might agree to pay for a barrel of oil (in say, three months) may be $52. (The futures price depends on how the market expects oil prices to change over the next three months and the level of interest rates, as well as storage costs.) With this agreement, you have the obligation to pay $52 for a barrel of oil in three months, and the counterparty is required to physically deliver the barrel of oil to you. Since most financial investors in commodities rarely want to actually receive the barrel of oil (and the other party normally doesn't want to deliver it to you), virtually all commodities futures contracts are settled before the predetermined delivery date. The settlement terms are simply the difference between the then-current price and the futures price that had been established at the inception of the contract. In the preceding example, if the price of oil is $55, then the winning party who purchased the commodity future earns $3 ($55 current price minus $52 agreed upon futures price), and the losing side that sold it pays $3. It is a zero-sum game because the gains of one party are equal to the losses of the other.

In practice, entering these futures contracts is simpler than it may seem at first. You do not actually have to go find someone who will take the other side and hire an attorney to draft the agreement. These contracts are actively traded in highly liquid regulated exchanges that are not too different from the stock and bond markets. Long-term investors, short-term speculators, and those who are looking to hedge themselves against adverse commodity price movements trade in these markets. The hedgers are typically commodity producers, who often prefer to lock in the price at which they are going to sell the commodity in the future, or corporate consumers looking to lock in their costs. These market participants can take both sides of the trade and together create sufficient buyers and sellers of commodity futures contracts to establish a fluid tradable market.

The second way to gain commodity exposure is to buy the stocks of the corporations that invest in the production of commodities such as those that mine for industrial or precious metals, extract energy (crude oil or natural gas), or produce agriculture. Since the profits of these companies can potentially be largely influenced by the price of the underlying commodity, the general price movement of the stock should also be correlated to the commodity price. Since stocks are liquid investments, you can gain exposure to commodity prices with little effort and none of the cumbersome restrictions that come with holding physical commodities.

The challenge with this approach is that the stock price may not be highly correlated with the underlying commodity price. The companies may be mismanaged or they may hedge out the price risk of the commodity, thereby potentially missing out on any upward commodity price movement. Another way to say this is that by investing in commodity stocks, you are taking on additional stock market risk on top of the risk of commodity price changes. Therefore, you may have periods during which the commodity price goes up but the stock price falls, and vice versa. Recall that the key to building a balanced portfolio is to ensure that the various economic environments are adequately covered. Thus, it is imperative that your commodity allocation track the price of the underlying commodities as closely as possible.

This can be accomplished by focusing on particular commodity equities that have historically demonstrated high correlation to shifting commodity prices for the particular sector in which they operate. Commodity companies can generally be classified by two broad categories that refer to the company's location in the supply chain: upstream and downstream. Companies involved in upstream production are the closest to the underlying commodity because they find, extract, or produce the raw materials. Downstream companies, in contrast, sell to the end consumer and are therefore a few steps removed from the underlying commodity value. As a result, upstream natural resource companies typically provide a tighter fit between the commodity price and the stock price. This means that a well-diversified upstream commodity-stock allocation could alleviate some, but not all, of the concerns with the equity exposure.

In summary, the challenge with investing in commodity futures is that the historical return has been very low for a long time (as will be demonstrated shortly). Although there are clear diversification benefits of including this asset class even with low returns, it's always better to achieve higher returns. One way to boost the return is to apply leverage (as we do with Treasuries and TIPS). Another is through the use of commodity equities, which in contrast, have delivered high, equity-like returns over the long run. The issue with commodity equities, however, is that they come with additional equity risk. We have already included equities in our risk parity portfolio, so we should be mindful of the potential overlap, particularly as it relates to the economic bias of the asset exposure.

Figure 6.1 compares the historic excess returns of commodity futures to commodity producer equities. I also show returns during good and bad environments.

Figure 6.1   Annualized Long-Term Commodity Futures and Commodity Producer Equities Excess Returns by Economic Environment – January 1970 to March 2021

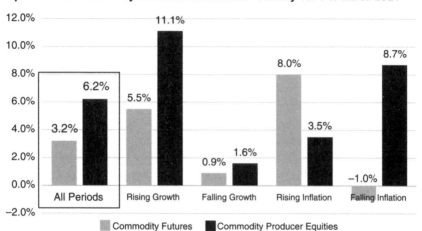

Source: Bloomberg. Methodology used to determine if growth and inflation are rising or falling: current growth or inflation rate compared to average of the trailing 12-month period. If the current rate (of growth/inflation) is higher, then that is considered a rising growth/ inflation period and vice versa. The logic is based on the observation that most people expect the future to closely resemble the recent trend line.

The numbers that stand out are the rising and falling inflation figures for commodity producer equities. This asset class actually outperformed during falling inflation since 1970 as the equity bias to falling inflation outweighed the commodity bias toward rising inflation. I will address this shortly.

WHAT IS THE BEST WAY TO INVEST IN COMMODITIES?

Choosing between commodity futures and commodity equities may seem easy based on the significant long-term return difference presented in Figure 6.1. In addition, commodity equities are much more tax-efficient vehicles than investing in commodity futures. In Chapter 4, I explained how Treasury futures are more tax efficient than Treasury bonds, because the income is taxed as ordinary income (which typically has the highest marginal federal tax rate). In the case of commodities, the opposite is true. As with Treasury futures, commodity futures are taxed at 60/40 long-term/ short-term capital-gains rates. The difference here is that the alternative is equities as opposed to bonds. Equities are inherently more tax efficient because the only tax paid while holding the asset class is on the dividend income, which is a small portion of the total return. Also, many dividends benefit from favorable qualified dividend tax treatment under the current code. Stocks may pay a dividend to shareholders, but the main reason to invest in equities is for capital appreciation, which is not taxed until the holder sells the position. In either case, it is important to balance across different commodity sectors and avoid overconcentration in energy – the largest and most volatile sector, which often dominates commodity producer or futures indices.

Based on higher potential returns and greater tax efficiency, there is a clear advantage to investing in commodity equities instead of commodity futures. However, we must be mindful about what we are ultimately trying to achieve from this process. The main goal is to gain exposure to this asset class and its economic biases to help us construct a well-balanced risk parity portfolio.

Both commodities and equities are rising growth assets. Equities do better with falling inflation, whereas commodities are rising-inflation biased. This poses two considerations. First, we need to make sure that the commodity allocation does not overly expose our total portfolio to rising growth. You can think of commodity equities as providing exposure to both commodities and equities. There is also some implicit leverage in the exposures since commodity companies are often levered entities (with leverage above the average for stocks), so the total exposure to stocks and commodities is probably greater than 100%. We need to take this into account when constructing our total commodity portfolio to avoid over-allocating to the rising growth economic exposure. Doing so would overly expose our risk parity portfolio to that particular economic outcome and leave us underexposed to the opposite environment. This means that our total portfolio would likely outperform during rising growth and underperform during falling growth. We should strive for better balance.

There appears to be a trade-off between using commodity futures and commodity equities. The former provide pure commodity exposure without incorporating additional unneeded equity risk. The latter have a higher expected return and are more tax efficient. The way to think about the dilemma is in the same terms that we seek to balance across: rising growth, falling growth, rising inflation, and falling inflation. The role of commodities is to cover the rising growth and rising inflation environments. The problem with commodity equities is twofold. First, it overexposes us to rising growth because of the leveraged exposure to stocks and commodities, both of which are biased to outperform during rising growth. Second, it underachieves the rising inflation target because commodities do well during rising inflation but stocks do not.

One way to potentially resolve these issues is to recalibrate the commodity equity allocation. If we can identify a commodity that is biased to outperform during falling growth, then that would allow us to reduce the exposure of the total commodity basket to rising growth. Moreover, we need to increase the inflation-hedging component to offset the falling inflation bias of the equity exposure. There is a simple solution that can accomplish both objectives.

The commodity asset class can be broken down into two subgroups: industrial commodities and gold. The reason to separate into these two types is because they have different biases to economic growth. Both are inflation hedges, but gold tends to perform better during falling growth periods, whereas all the other commodities are biased to outperform during rising growth environments.

The reason for the distinction is that gold is more of a currency and storehold of wealth. Other commodities like copper, aluminum, crude oil, natural gas, and livestock are items that are consumed. As a result, their price is largely impacted by rising and falling demand, which is, in turn, heavily influenced by economic growth. Gold, on the other hand, is not used for much outside of producing expensive jewelry. The majority of its demand is derived from its status as a currency and store of value for thousands of years. Gold can also serve as a safe haven asset to which investors may flock during a crisis, which often occurs amid an economic downturn.

The year 2008 provides a good example of the difference in growth bias between gold and industrial commodity equities. The Morningstar Global Upstream Natural Resources Total Return Index is a diversified basket of commodity producer stocks that is split across energy, metals, agriculture, water, and timber. In 2008, the index dropped 45% as economic growth unexpectedly tumbled, inflation fell, and momentarily resulted in deflation, and there was widespread panic as the global economy collapsed. This environment presents the perfect storm for broad commodities, which are generally biased to outperform in the exact opposite economic climate (of rising growth and inflation). Gold, however, was up about 6% for the year, while the other commodities suffered. The same outcome resulted in the first quarter of 2020 when COVID-19 halted the global economy. The commodity index plunged 31% in three months while gold gained 4%.

Gold is also a good hedge against the debasement of currency through quantitative easing. Since gold has established itself as the oldest currency in the world and has a finite supply, whenever more dollars, euros, or yen are created and placed into circulation, the price of gold per unit of paper money should theoretically rise. Other commodity prices may also benefit from quantitative easing because they are real assets, but the connection is looser than it is with gold. Also, the price of industrial commodities is heavily influenced by rising and falling demand and shifting supply, further reducing the direct impact of quantitative easing to its price. The supply of gold, however, is relatively fixed, and has generally increased at a slow annual rate as new gold gets mined. The current widespread use of quantitative easing as a monetary policy tool has increased the potential upside of gold.

By splitting between commodity producer equities and gold bullion, we are able to assemble a total commodity basket that achieves our overall objective of maintaining a high expected return and the desired economic bias of rising growth and rising inflation. By splitting the total commodity basket 60% in industrial commodity equities (excluding gold mining companies) and 40% in gold, we are able to balance the full commodity allocation to achieve the desired exposure of rising inflation and rising growth without overallocating to either environment. Think of it this way: the falling growth bias of gold helps offset the overexposure to rising growth that comes from a double allocation to commodity prices and equity risk (from the commodity equities). Likewise, the strong rising inflation bias of gold helps offset some of the falling inflation bias of the equity exposure.

Commodity equities plus gold can combine to form a very efficient way to achieve the target total commodity exposure. Additionally, the mix of the two has a higher expected return and is much more tax efficient than using commodity futures alone. Since 1970, gold has earned 2.9% annualized excess returns only trailing global stocks by 1.1% per year (as a point of reference). Finally, this approach allows for easier implementation since commodity stocks and gold (through an exchange-traded fund) are readily accessible to nearly all investors.

Figure 6.2 summarizes the historical returns for this 60/40 mix and compares the results to commodity futures. I present the returns during all environments, as well as performance during the various economic climates.

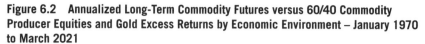

Figure 6.2   Annualized Long-Term Commodity Futures versus 60/40 Commodity Producer Equities and Gold Excess Returns by Economic Environment – January 1970 to March 2021

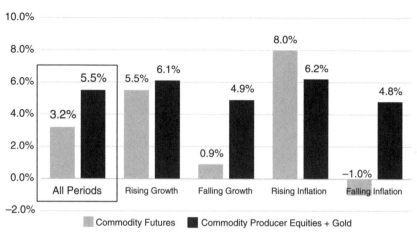

Source: Bloomberg. Methodology used to determine if growth and inflation are rising or falling: current growth or inflation rate compared to average of the trailing 12-month period. If the current rate (of growth/inflation) is higher, then that is considered a rising growth/inflation period and vice versa. The logic is based on the observation that most people expect the future to closely resemble the recent trend line.

Note that the 60/40 mix offers attractive return characteristics when compared to the commodity futures allocation. It has a higher historical (and expected) return and, most important, it provides the desired exposure during rising inflation and rising growth economic environments that we didn't achieve with commodity producer equities alone.

OTHER CONSIDERATIONS

One potential roadblock for commodity investing is its potential impact on the environment. Sustainable investing has been gaining steam and is becoming more closely scrutinized. Additionally, there are growing concerns about the long-term sustainability of certain commodities like fossil fuels and coal that may damage the environment. There is a clear movement toward environmentally conscious consumption including replacing cars fueled by gas with electric vehicles, which may continue to curtail the demand for certain commodities. This secular trend may pose a headwind for prices over time, although it's not clear how this pressure nets out since the transition to renewables will take time and has also led and will lead to underinvestment in fossil fuel production in the interim, which may push prices higher. However, just as shifting consumer preferences and environmental regulation may challenge some commodities such as fossil fuels, other commodities may benefit from the other side of these trends. For example, demand for copper is expected to increase due to its extensive use in electric vehicles and batteries.

Some investors may opt to own a smaller allocation in less sustainable commodities in exchange for a more meaningful exposure to clean energy or mining that may actually benefit from the same secular forces. It is not clear which will outperform over time, so this is more of an investor preference.

SUMMARY

Commodity equities plus gold (60/40 split) have delivered comparable returns to equities over the past 50 years and offer strong diversification benefits. Commodities are traditionally heavily underowned in portfolios. This is particularly true for high-net-worth individuals. Sophisticated institutional investors including endowments and pension funds tend to have a higher percentage of their portfolios in natural resource companies.

Inflation pressures may ultimately emerge amid excessive quantitative easing. Additionally, near zero interest rates across most of the developed world could encourage spending cash that is earning meager returns. These forces could result in growing inflation pressures over time, which further supports the need to include commodities in a well-diversified portfolio.

CHAPTER SEVEN

Other Asset Classes

In prior chapters, I introduced you to four major asset classes: equities, Treasuries, TIPS, and commodities. These asset classes were carefully selected because of their unique bias to various growth and inflation outcomes. A portfolio only consisting of these asset classes may be considered well diversified because the four major economic environments are covered. That said, incorporating additional asset classes could be further diversifying and beneficial to the portfolio. The key step in the analysis is to think of each asset class under consideration within the same framework that has been established to this point: What is the asset class's bias to rising/falling growth and inflation? The cause-effect relationship understanding is critical to maintaining a balanced allocation that is not overly sensitive to any particular economic outcome.

In this chapter I will present various popular asset classes beyond the ones already discussed that I have seen included in institutional and high-net-worth portfolios. The economic bias of each asset class will be explored as well as its potential diversification benefit relative to the four major market segments already included in our risk parity portfolio.

As a reminder and guide in this initial process, Table 7.1 provides a summary of the economic biases of each of the four asset classes covered up to now. More important, the reasoning behind each bias is included. You need to possess a strong grasp *of the rationale* in order to effectively apply the same logic to new asset classes.

Table 7.1   The Economic Bias of Four Major Asset Classes

Asset Class	Growth	Rationale	Inflation	Rationale
Equities	Rising	Higher company revenues	Falling	Lower input costs, cheaper financing
Long-Term Treasuries	Falling	Falling interest rates to stimulate economy	Falling	Falling interest rates to increase inflation
Long-Term TIPS	Falling	Falling interest rates to stimulate economy	Rising	Pays inflation rate
Commodities– Industrial	Rising	Rising demand for commodities	Rising	Higher commodity prices part of inflation measure
Commodities– Gold	Falling	Safe haven, QE hedge	Rising	Hedge against monetary inflation

EQUITY SUBGROUPS

The most popular asset class is equities. This asset class dominates investment news headlines and can be found in the vast majority of portfolios. The chapter that addressed this market assumed broad market exposure that invested across the vast majority of listed public companies around the world.

Many market participants prefer to slice up equities into smaller subsegments. For instance, a common distinction is made between growth and value or large and small capitalization companies. The total equity pie can also be sliced by sector such as technology, financials, or healthcare.

A common oversight of investors is the false sense of feeling well diversified because they own many equity funds. Although these segments do experience some divergence of returns over time, their general economic biases to growth and inflation are similar to those of the broad global equity market. The cause-effect connection makes sense because groups of public companies, whether large or small, generate profits similarly as they relate to the general economic climate and are all subject to the business cycle to varying degrees. Likewise, the earnings for growth- and value-oriented companies, for the most part, are driven by similar forces when considered within the context of broad economic trends.

Equities could also be divided into groups that are more directly linked to either growth or inflation factors. For example, you may be able to find a subsegment of equities that are more hedged against rising inflation than the average public company. There may be certain industries that are better able to pass through cost increases to their customers and may therefore be less sensitive to rising inflation headwinds. Likewise, some types of companies have historically withstood weak economic environments better than others.

All these distinctions within the equity market may be valid, but they may only make a small difference. If you do identify an equity subsegment that you are confident can withstand (and better yet, appreciate) during rising inflation and weak economic periods in the future, then you are free to plug it into your portfolio. You just need to make sure you account for it correctly when determining its economic bias. This is what I have found with commodity producer equities and why we separate out that particular market segment. The key is proper categorization.

Also, recognize that the analysis goes both ways. If you decide to only hold stocks that are biased to perform better during weak economic periods, during rising inflationary times, or both, then you leave yourself exposed to the opposite environment: If the economy is very strong, then your stocks may not keep up with the market. More important, the gains may be insufficient to make up for the underperformance elsewhere in your balanced portfolio. Again, the key is to ensure that you have balanced it appropriately and that comes from categorizing it correctly at the outset. And it's important to recognize that, in most cases, equities are more similar to each other than they are different, so an equity-focused approach to diversification may result in underdiversification over the long run.

NON-US BONDS

The bond allocations we have referenced thus far only include investments in US sovereign fixed income (Treasuries and TIPS). Investors have the option to also invest in bonds issued by non-US entities. Moving the bond exposure outside the country can provide additional diversification benefits, because US bonds may do well at certain times while non-US fixed income may underperform and vice versa. While high-quality non-US bonds have the same economic bias as US Treasuries (falling growth and falling inflation), the returns may differ since each is biased toward its own country's economic conditions, which may diverge at times. Of course, global economic conditions may ultimately influence cross-border flows and trade due to international ties, but the potential for some diversification still remains over time.

There is also the opportunity to diversify the currency in which the bond portfolio is invested. Investing across multiple currencies reduces the risk of being concentrated in a single currency that may suffer a prolonged bear market. That said, I generally prefer a home country bias in currency holdings for two main reasons. First, expenses and liabilities are typically denominated in one's home currency. If you live in the United States and you spend US dollars, then that is the currency to which you must eventually convert your investments. You may be less concerned about whether the dollar appreciates or depreciates, because you are going to spend dollars in either case. If you convert your money into euros and the euro falls, then you take an actual dollar hit when viewed in US dollar terms. A falling home currency may be more problematic from an inflation, rather than a currency, perspective. This is because anything that is imported into your home country may cost more due to a weaker local currency. We can address this risk by investing in a diverse mix of asset classes biased to outperform during rising inflation such as commodities, gold, and TIPS.

The other potential issue with owning non-US bonds of developed economies is the volatility of foreign currencies. This is particularly concerning when interest rates are low around the globe, because the currency volatility can dominate the total return. Importantly, the long-term expected return of any single developed market currency trade is zero. This means that investors are not compensated for the risk over the long run. There is a diversification benefit that shouldn't be underestimated, but it is informative to recognize that there is little or no enhanced expected return contribution to the total portfolio from holding outside currencies.

Bonds issued by emerging markets – in contrast to developed nations – may offer some unique diversification benefits. To start, they typically come with a higher yield than US Treasuries and other developed economy sovereign bonds because they are considered riskier. Emerging economies have historically failed to pay back their lenders more frequently than the United States, which has never defaulted on its bonds. The risk across emerging markets can vary greatly due to differences in credit, social, currency, and political risks that exist among countries.

In order to determine the appropriate environmental bias of emerging market bonds, some understanding of these economies and how they generally differ from developed nations is required. Many of these developing countries are able to expand their economies by taking advantage of demand that comes from outside their borders. By definition, these are economies that are in an early phase of their maturation periods and that are working toward becoming fully developed countries. Therefore, much of their growth comes from selling abroad to wealthier countries rather than to domestic consumers. Goods, services, and commodities are produced in emerging markets and exported to richer nations. Based on this, the growth and inflation dynamics that support these factors tend to benefit emerging markets. However, the analysis is more complex because there are potential cross-currents.

Local emerging market bonds can be split into the underlying bonds in local currency and the currency itself. The bonds in local currency, like Treasuries, are biased to do better during periods characterized by falling growth and falling inflation. However, the currency generally has the opposite bias of rising growth and is mixed with respect to rising or falling inflation. Stronger growth is a positive outcome because that normally leads to more purchases of the goods, services, and commodities that these countries sell to the rest of the world and investments in their economies. This demand can result in inflows into the currency causing it to appreciate. Conversely, during falling growth environments, some emerging markets may suffer from a balance-of-payments crisis that results from capital fleeing the economy that can cause the currency to depreciate. Rising inflation could be good or bad for the currency. Inflation devalues currencies on a relative basis versus other currencies. If inflation were rising in the United States and not in the emerging market, that would benefit the emerging market currency, but typically when inflation has risen in the United States it has risen much more in the emerging market.

The net economic bias of the asset class is less clear since it depends on how the price movements of the local bonds relate to the shifts in currency and which force is greater at a particular point in time. In fact, the currencies are often much more volatile than the bonds themselves, thereby dominating the total return to investors. Additionally, there should be a distinction made between commodity exporters – whose economies, currencies, and ability to repay hard foreign exchange debt benefit from rising commodity prices – and noncommodity exporters who may not enjoy similar tailwinds. I have often seen emerging-market bonds as an asset class outperform during periods associated with rising inflation, which may be particularly useful to a risk parity portfolio given the lack of available inflation hedges. I have also observed losses during falling growth periods as capital flows out of the emerging market bonds and into Treasuries as a safe haven.

All in all, we need to consider potential complexities that come with liquidity, availability, and taxation of foreign bonds. In our risk parity portfolio, I assume no international bonds in an effort to maintain a simple, liquid, and tax-efficient allocation. That said, this is one area that we continue to explore and analyze as a possible investment option in an effort to improve diversification and potentially increase the expected return. This may particularly be the case if US interest rates continue their downward trajectory of the past 40 years and again approach near zero (like much of the developed world). At that point, there may be a need to diversify into emerging market bonds of countries like China, which may hold up better during a downside growth scenario because their yields have more room to fall, offering greater potential price appreciation.

CORPORATE BONDS

Another variety of fixed income includes bonds issued by corporations, rather than by governments. These loans are considered less safe, because they are not backed by the full faith and credit of the government (which also controls the printing presses). Due to their greater risk of default, or credit risk, these bonds should offer a superior yield over Treasuries. This is particularly true for bonds that have a lower credit rating, which indicates a greater risk of default. A few companies are rated AAA, meaning that their debt is considered very safe. These high-quality bonds have a much lower yield, which is closer to that of Treasuries to reflect the relatively high probability of being repaid principal. Companies rated BB and below are termed high-yield, or junk bonds because they often come with a higher yield to compensate investors for the greater risk of default.

Corporate bonds are often quoted in terms of a credit spread, which is the difference between their yield and that of Treasuries (the risk-free rate). Generally, the greater the odds of default, the higher the credit spread. The credit spread is effectively the excess return that investors demand for taking on the risk of default. This is the same concept that I've covered in prior chapters when comparing the expected returns of each asset class to the returns offered by risk-free cash. Treasuries are used here instead of cash in order to match the duration of the bonds and simplify the math.

Corporate bonds can be viewed as part Treasury-like and part equity-like. The return of corporate bonds will be impacted by shifts in the risk-free rate (prices rise as interest rates fall and vice versa) as well as changes in credit spreads. We can observe how the risk-free and spread components perform in different economic environments and how those biases net out to determine its economic bias. The lower the credit quality, the more corporate bonds act like equities, because the impact of moving credit spreads influences the total return more than changes in interest rates. The lower the quality of the debt, the greater the risk of default and the more the overall risk will be driven by the borrower's ability to repay the debt (which is better during rising growth than falling growth).

Treasuries do well during falling growth (and falling inflationary) periods. Corporate bonds, on the other hand, may outperform during rising growth (particularly lower-quality bonds). Like Treasuries, they are biased to do better during falling inflationary outcomes; however, unlike Treasuries, they can get absolutely crushed if inflation falls too much and nears deflationary levels. You should note that even though corporate bonds may seem more like Treasuries, they often share the same economic biases as equities. Although they are technically bonds, they can act more like stocks. Corporate bonds are a claim on the cash flows of the companies that issue them. They are less risky than stocks because they come before stocks in the priority of cash flows (bondholders are paid fist, then stockholders). Nevertheless, they are subject to the same corporate cash flows and the economic conditions that drive them.

You now have the knowledge and tools to determine on your own what factors ultimately result in improved conditions for corporate bonds. These debt securities yield more than Treasuries of equivalent duration because of the greater risk of default. Thus, it makes sense that these bonds would fare better whenever the odds of default go down. Stronger economic growth clearly makes it more likely that the company will not default because its profits are biased to improve (just as is the case when thinking about the economic bias of stocks). In addition, falling inflation is a positive outcome for corporate bonds just as it is for stocks, because it reduces borrowing expenses and input costs, further increasing profit margins. With this logic, it should be clear why deflation would be so bad for corporate bonds. Corporate earnings would likely collapse in a deflationary environment, which makes it less likely that a company will repay its debt holders. Treasuries, in contrast, outperform during this environment because of the lack of credit risk.

MUNICIPAL BONDS

Municipal bonds are debt obligations issued by states and local government entities. Investors who pay taxes are typically attracted to municipal bonds because they have the rare advantage of having interest income that is tax-free. These bonds are typically exempt from federal taxes and, under certain conditions, state and potentially local taxes.

Municipal bonds have some common characteristics with Treasuries. Higher-quality, higher-rated municipal bonds are comparable to Treasuries. These bonds are considered fairly safe because they are backed by entities that have historically exhibited fairly low default rates and have the ability to raise taxes to pay their debts. In fact, municipal bonds normally offer even lower yields than Treasuries because of their tax advantage (note that Treasuries are federally taxable). High-quality municipal bonds are widely considered a more tax-efficient version of the risk-free asset and therefore have the fundamental bias to outperform during falling growth and falling inflation environments (like Treasuries).

Municipal bonds with lower ratings and higher yields, however, can behave more like corporate bonds than Treasuries. As a result, lower-quality municipal bonds are slightly more biased to outperform during rising growth and falling inflation environments than higher-quality municipal bonds.

COMMERCIAL REAL ESTATE

Commercial real estate includes sectors such as office, industrial, retail, and multifamily (apartments). Investors can access commercial real estate investments either in public or private structures. Public real estate investment trusts (REITs) are traded stocks that buy, sell, develop, and manage real estate. The vast majority of their profits are distributed to their shareholders in accordance with regulations. The attractiveness of REITs is that they offer investors the opportunity to easily gain exposure to commercial real estate without giving up liquidity. The drawback is similar to that of commodity producer equities. You not only gain exposure to the underlying investments (real estate in this case) but also to the associated stock market risks. Consequently, the returns of REITs are impacted both by general changes in commercial real estate conditions as well as broad stock market moves. Private real estate, on the other hand, involves a direct investment in commercial buildings such as apartments, industrial buildings, and office and retail properties. By investing in the buildings, you can gain a direct link to commercial real estate prices but give up the liquidity advantages of public-traded REITs.

The environmental bias of commercial real estate in terms of economic growth is relatively straightforward. Rising growth is a positive outcome because of the greater support to increase rents because stronger economic growth generally results in higher incomes and growing corporate profits. Improved incomes allow apartment tenants the financial ability to pay higher rents for better-quality housing. Higher corporate profits enable businesses to pay for more commercial space to expand. From a high level, improving economic conditions generally produce increasing demand for commercial real estate properties, which also exerts upward pressure on prices. In this sense, real estate behaves similarly to equities and may be less diversifying than is commonly thought.

The inflationary bias of real estate is less straightforward. On one side, real estate could be considered an inflation hedge. Land and buildings are real assets with a relatively inelastic supply that should benefit from generally rising prices. This is particularly true because of the long lead time required to develop new properties. However, there is a competing force that makes real estate biased to outperform during falling inflationary environments. Real estate is commonly acquired using debt, because most real estate transactions are not 100% cash purchases. Falling inflation generally leads to lower interest rates, which effectively makes real estate more affordable from a financing standpoint. Conversely, rising inflation often corresponds to higher interest rates, creating a headwind for real estate affordability. All else being equal, it costs more to buy real estate as the rate of interest goes up. Higher financing costs also negatively impact your net profit in real estate, as one of the biggest expenses is the cost of interest on a mortgage. In addition, higher commodities prices can increase construction costs for new developments. And longer-term leases – which are effectively bonds – decline in value, since their rents are relatively fixed and typically do not rise with inflation or, if they do, may do so with a material lag. In sum, there are multiple variables that affect the sensitivity of commercial real estate to shifts in inflation, so the net results are mixed, largely depending on the particular type of real estate in question – including how quickly cash flows can adjust to rising inflation.

PRIVATE EQUITY

Private equity refers to privately held companies. This is in contrast to pub-licly traded stocks. Both are investments in the equity of companies, with the main difference being the liquidity and pricing (stocks price daily). Some investors categorize private equity as an alternative investment, sug-gesting that it is a completely different type of asset class. The reality is that public and private equity are quite similar in terms of their behavior, even though you may not see it day to day (because the price of private equity is not marked to the prevailing market price on a daily basis).

Therefore, this asset class is very easy to categorize: it is a rising-growth, falling-inflation asset, just like public equities. This is a long-term assessment since the price is typically only updated a few times a year (and just because accounting statements have not been updated, that does not mean values have not changed). Notwithstanding the illiquid nature of private equity, the underlying fundamentals of the companies represented are impacted by shifting growth and inflation conditions, just as are pub-lic companies.

HEDGE FUNDS

Contrary to popular usage, hedge funds are actually not an asset class. The term *hedge funds* covers a wide array of investment strategies. The term *hedge fund* refers merely to the structure of these funds, just as mutual funds or exchange traded funds refer to different investment structures. The actual investments that can be found inside hedge funds vary greatly. In practice, the majority of hedge funds tend to be highly correlated to stocks. In essence, a minority of hedge funds actually meaningfully hedge, leaving them with long market exposure to equities and credit. Therefore, the broad economic bias of this group of investments is rising growth and falling inflation. Of course, there are many exceptions, given the broad diversity of strategies in this space. Each strategy needs to be analyzed individually and assessed on its own merits and in light of its historical performance.

I believe that certain low-correlation hedge fund strategies can be a useful tool in building portfolios, but this is outside the scope of our risk parity portfolio. By definition, *low correlation* means that these strategies do not have a general economic bias. This suggests that they may be useful in combination with a risk parity allocation, but they do not have a role within the risk parity portfolio itself.

CRYPTOCURRENCIES

Perhaps the most hotly debated emerging asset class is cryptocurrency. Some view versions of this new digital currency like Bitcoin as competing with gold. Bitcoin has even taken on the label of "digital gold" in some circles. The idea is that in a world of continual quantitative easing and a system of fiat currency, alternative storeholds of wealth that cannot be debased due to finite supply (like gold) seem relatively attractive. This is particularly true when designing a balanced portfolio that should persist through time.

Relative to gold, which has been considered a currency for thousands of years, cryptocurrency is a relatively new concept. Bitcoin, the first cryptocurrency, was created in 2009. The technological innovation backing the currency is known as blockchain. From a simplistic standpoint, you can think of this invention like a publicly available locked Excel spreadsheet that lists every cryptocurrency transaction. Since everyone can see it and verify the data, it cannot be corrupted or tampered with. There is also a finite supply of the currency, limiting concerns about debasement. Finally, the currency trades on an exchange, so its current value can be easily observed. It is a remarkable invention, yet it is relatively new. The price is highly volatile since many of the early investors are speculators. Over time, it is very possible that institutional ownership will increase, helping to stabilize the price and improving the long-term viability of Bitcoin and potentially other cryptocurrencies.

There is a particular attraction to cryptocurrency in the current environment. A mandatory foundation for any currency is trust. Owners of the money must firmly believe that it will continue indefinitely to hold its value as currency. There are a few dimensions to consistent value. One big draw to some cryptocurrencies like Bitcoin is the promised finite supply.

One of the biggest risks of any currency is the potential for its creator to increase the quantity of money, which dilutes the value for existing owners. Imagine if the government suddenly decided to send every American *but you* a $1 billion check by creating new US dollars to raise the needed funds. What would that do to the value of the currency you hold? Would the median home price in the United States still be around $250,000 or would it go up significantly since there are far more dollars in circulation relative to the supply of homes? Your money would instantly become worthless because of dilution. You still have the same dollars, but its purchasing power has completely diminished. This is an extreme example to make the point that a risk we all take with currency is debasement.

Since 2008, trillions of dollars of new money have been injected in response to the severe economic weakness first caused by the Great Financial Crisis and then the COVID-19 pandemic. It is no coincidence that during this period, alternate currencies such as gold and cryptocurrencies have materially appreciated. Investors have been clamoring for forms of money that cannot be printed and debased. The rapid ascent of cryptocurrency, particularly Bitcoin, stands out in this regard.

One major issue with this asset class is that the causal relationship between the environment and cryptocurrency returns is not as obvious as it is with gold. The main reason for this is that cryptocurrencies are still a new asset class and being fully adopted can take years if not decades. In the early stages, there tend to be more speculation with investors jumping in during bull markets and fleeing amid significant price declines, which means that the current growth bias of cryptocurrencies is less clear. Over time, the investor base may solidify and the volatility reduce. At some point in the future, I may consider the leading cryptocurrencies at the time as a diversifier to gold if they demonstrate a comparable economic bias but still offer diversification benefits.

CASH

We spend cash, and all investments must ultimately be converted back to cash, whether in electronic or physical form, before the value of the assets can be used to purchase something. In this respect, cash is a currency and provides the needed liquidity to pay for goods and services. For purposes of considering cash as a strategic asset class to which we target a percentage of our long-term portfolio, the analysis moves beyond the core purpose of cash as a spending currency.

Cash has long been considered one of the major asset classes. As of this writing, cash was yielding zero. However, the long-term average yield of cash is closer to 4%, which would make it a more viable consideration for inclusion in portfolios. In fact, many portfolios tend to hold cash as a strategic long-term holding. A permanent position in this asset class is typically justified by one of two rationales. First, cash can serve as dry powder that may be deployed at opportune times, when markets fall and may present attractive entry points. The other appealing characteristic of cash is that its value is generally stable and in certain rare environments it may be the best-performing asset class.

I prefer not to hold cash as part of the risk parity portfolio. Cash is widely considered to be the risk-free asset and therefore offers a guaranteed return for those not seeking higher returns. In other words, you can take zero risk and earn whatever yield cash delivers (0% today and 4% on average over the past century). All other risky asset classes are expected to outperform cash over the long run. Again, there would be no reason for anyone to take the risk associated with the other asset classes if they did not expect to be compensated for the potential of losing money.

A diversified portfolio represents an attempt to outperform cash over the long run while minimizing risk. The way I try to do this using a risk parity framework is by investing across a diverse set of asset classes, each biased to outperform in various economic environments, which is the main driver of asset-class returns.

As such, I think of cash as sitting outside of a balanced allocation. Cash serves the purpose of covering any liquidity needs but should not be included in the long-term asset allocation, because it will reduce the long-term expected return. Thus, when I am discussing the risk parity portfolio, I exclude cash since I am effectively trying to beat cash with controlled risk over the long run. By putting it into the portfolio we merely dilute the long-term return benefits of the other asset classes. Note that cash may show up in the portfolio as collateral for a Treasury futures holding, but it is not there as an asset-class target allocation.

SUMMARY

Table 7.2 offers a summary of the economic sensitivity of all the asset classes discussed earlier. Most importantly, it provides the rationale for the economic bias of each.

Diversification across assets biased to outperform during various economic environments is the hallmark of our risk parity portfolio. From this perspective, additional diverse asset classes can be included in a well-balanced asset allocation to improve the return to risk ratio of the

Table 7.2   The Economic Bias of Major Asset Classes (Expanded List)

Asset Class	Growth	Rationale	Inflation	Rationale
Public/Private Equity	Rising	Higher company revenues	Falling	Lower input costs, cheaper financing
Long-Term Global Sovereign Bonds/ High-Quality Municipal Bonds	Falling	Falling interest rates to stimulate economy	Falling	Falling interest rates to increase inflation
Long-Term TIPS	Falling	Falling interest rates to stimulate economy	Rising	Pays inflation rate
Commodities– Industrial	Rising	Rising demand for commodities	Rising	Higher commodity prices part of inflation measure
Commodities– Gold	Falling	Safe haven, QE hedge	Rising	Hedge against monetary inflation
Cryptocurrency	Too soon to know		Too soon to know	
High-Yield Corporate Bonds	Rising	Higher company revenues	Falling	Lower input costs, cheaper financing
Emerging Market Bonds	Mixed	Pos: Higher country revenues Neg: Rising interest rates	Rising/Mixed	Higher revenues due to higher price of items exported
Commercial Real Estate	Rising	Higher rents, greater demand	Mixed	Pos: Real asset Neg: Higher interest rates
Hedge Funds	Rising/Mixed	Generally overweight equity and credit risk	Falling/Mixed	Generally overweight equity and credit risk

total portfolio. This chapter introduced you to several additional asset classes that you may consider for your allocation. Certainly, new investments will also come to market in the future, just as TIPS came into existence in the late 1990s. The key is to appreciate in what environment the asset class is biased to do well and poorly and construct a portfolio through that lens.

For the purposes of our risk parity portfolio, I will limit our allocation to global equities, Treasuries, TIPS, and commodities (split into industrial commodity equities and gold). In the following chapters I will dive into the process of constructing a risk parity portfolio using these four major asset classes.

CHAPTER EIGHT

Risk Parity
Portfolio Summary

I begin this chapter by zooming out for a moment and recapping what I've covered thus far. There are two key steps to constructing a well-diversified risk parity portfolio:

1. Select diverse asset classes to reduce risk.
2. Structure each to have comparable returns.

I walked you through the asset classes that I have chosen and why. I include global equities, Treasuries, TIPS, and commodities (industrial and gold) in our risk parity portfolio because they are biased to outperform during varying economic environments. Each of these four asset classes is predisposed to do well in either a rising or falling growth and inflation climate. Critically, I equally cover the four potential economic outcomes with these asset classes. Two asset classes do well during falling growth and two during rising growth. Similarly, two are biased to outperform when inflation is rising and two when it is falling. This symmetry is important because it allows us to more easily balance the allocation in the steps detailed below.

I also devoted time to describing how each of these asset classes can be structured to offer a long-term expected return that is in line with equities.

Equities do not need any special treatment as they obviously can deliver attractive long-term results. For commodities, I invest in commodity producer equities and gold, which offer higher expected returns than commodity futures. For TIPS and Treasuries, I opt to hold longer-duration bonds and employ modest amounts of leverage to increase the expected return (and risk) to a comparable level as equities.

These two steps leave us with four diverse asset classes, each of which has a similar expected return and risk over the long run. By combining assets biased to outperform during various economic environments, we have the opportunity to build a portfolio that can earn equity-like returns over the long term with less risk than equities because of its superior diversification characteristics.

We now need to put everything together to come up with our final target allocation to each asset class. This will represent our risk parity portfolio.

CONCEPTUAL FRAMEWORK

We strive to build a balanced allocation, which we define as a total portfolio unbiased to any particular economic outcome. We want it to perform about the same over time during rising growth periods as well as falling growth environments. In my experience, most portfolios are clearly biased to outperform during rising growth. We also wish for it to be indifferent to whether inflation is rising or falling. The vast majority of portfolios tend to be better off during falling inflation periods than the opposite. Both of these tendencies exist because the majority of conventional portfolios are predominantly exposed to equity and credit risk.

How do we build balanced exposure with the assets that we have described? I approach addressing the important allocation decision by thinking in terms of *direction* and *magnitude*. I have already established that each asset class will experience favorable and unfavorable economic environments. This covers the direction part of the equation – stocks do better with rising growth and worse with falling growth, TIPS have the opposite bias, and so on.

Direction is not enough to get us to balance. We also must consider the volatility of each asset class to determine the approximate magnitude of returns. Volatility is traditionally considered a measure of risk. The more volatile an asset class the riskier it is and vice versa. Interestingly, when we approach the problem from a risk parity angle, volatility can serve as a powerful diversification tool that has certain benefits that could be easily overlooked.

Volatility is typically expressed in terms of standard deviation of returns. Consider an asset class that earns 8% per year returns and has an average standard deviation of 15%. This statistical measure indicates that about two-thirds of the time, the return over one year falls between one standard deviation of its average. That is, about two-thirds of the time the return is between 23% and −7% (8% average plus 15% and minus 15%). The range within two standard deviations (38% and −22%) covers about 95% of the periods and three standard deviations (53% and −37%) approximately 99% of the time. These are mere statistical measures of historical returns and should not be construed as precise predictions about the future. We've all witnessed events that have fallen outside the normal bell-shaped distribution curve, having occurred more often than would have been expected based on standard deviation. For our purposes, standard deviation merely serves as a way to generally determine the volatility of an asset class.

In terms of factoring in volatility into the construction of our risk parity portfolio, the key is to appreciate that each asset class has an expected volatility around its mean. During favorable economic outcomes, the asset class is anticipated to outperform its average and vice versa. The more volatile the asset class the greater the magnitude of outperformance and underperformance relative to its average. As an example, let's consider that the asset class of stocks has historically had an average excess return of 5% and standard deviation of 15%. In a year supported by moderate levels of rising growth and/or falling inflation (a favorable environment for equities), stocks may earn 15% above cash (or 10% greater than an average year). In a moderately poor environment, they may deliver −5% (or 10% below average). In a terrific environment the excess returns would likely be higher at, say, 35% and would likely be hugely negative in a terrible environment. The magnitude of the swings around the average is directly related to the volatility of the asset class – the more volatile, the greater the dispersion relative to the average.

Let's compare stocks to a different asset class – namely, TIPS. To illustrate the point, we are going to use *short-term* TIPS in this example (note that we use long-term TIPS in our risk parity portfolio for reasons that will become apparent shortly). Let's assume the average historical excess return is 1.5% and the standard deviation 5%. You may notice that both the excess return and risk are about one-third that of equities. TIPS, as we've discussed, have the exact opposite economic bias of equities: falling growth and rising inflation.

If we experience a moderately favorable period for TIPS, then, instead of an average of 1.5%, they may deliver 6% above cash. In a bad year you may get 3% below cash. Since the standard deviation is relatively low, the dispersions around the average are small. This is what it means to have low volatility. In a really great period, you may see performance only slightly above the average. In short, the returns simply don't jump around much year over year regardless of what happens.

On a stand-alone basis, this return to risk profile may sound desirable. However, the level of returns is not attractive on an absolute basis, and within the context of building a well-balanced allocation, the low level of risk is not as beneficial. This is because *we need the asset classes to balance against one another to help us achieve a more consistent total portfolio return.* If the TIPS don't appreciate enough when equities are performing poorly, then the portfolio would be overly exposed to the environments during which equities are biased to do well. The goal, again, is to construct an allocation that is neutral to the economic outcome. As such, we should keep an eye on the impact to the total portfolio as opposed to the relative attractiveness of each individual asset class.

Therefore, we should strive to allocate *equal risk* to each economic environment. This means that the impact to the total portfolio should be roughly the same regardless of the environmental outcome. Taking our previous example, if the volatility and expected return for TIPS happened to be the same as equities, then that would provide a greater potential for good balance. When equities do poorly and underperform their average, TIPS should outperform their average since they have the opposite economic bias (both in terms of growth and inflation). On a total portfolio basis, the two would theoretically offset to yield a return closer to the average of the two. Importantly, in our updated example, the magnitude of the returns from both equities and TIPS should be about the same since they have comparable volatility.

The same thought process applies to the other asset classes. We actually prefer *more* volatility than less in this regard. This can be counterintuitive since it seems natural to generally opt for less risk versus more risk. When viewing the decision through the lens of building a well-balanced allocation of asset classes, however, the decision-making process is different.

A critical point is that none of this is intended to be precise. It would be a mistake to try to take these concepts and try to optimize a result by making assumptions of precision that are unreliable. History and past data may serve as a guide but should not be overly depended on and used to attempt optimization. The conceptual framework endures through time more so than the precise figures since the future will certainly be different from the past. That is, we can be more confident about the direction and rough magnitude of price moves of various asset classes during varying economic environments than we can of the exact changes.

Note also that the asset-class returns do not offset to zero over time, but rather, to the average of the underlying asset classes. This is an important point that is often overlooked. Many investors assume that when one asset is outperforming and another is underperforming, that means they essentially offset one another to break even. For instance, the thinking goes, if equities rise by 5% and commodities fall by 5%, then the net result is zero. However, this is not how it works. It is more accurate to say that both equities and commodities have an average long-term return that is greater than cash (otherwise investors would not invest in them since they can get the risk-free return of cash without risk). When equities underperform their average during a bad period and commodities outperform during a favorable environment for that asset class, then the two should net out closer to the long-term *positive average* of stocks and commodities rather than zero.

Remember, all asset classes offer a risk premium over cash. In a simple sense, the goal of risk parity investing is to capture this risk premium while balancing out the environmental biases of the asset classes, resulting in the smoothest possible path of returns.

TARGET ALLOCATION

Now that we have the four asset classes in our risk parity portfolio, the key question is what percentage do we allocate to each? Based on the framework established earlier, we are ready to take a few simple steps to determine the balanced allocation to our four asset classes. We begin with the long-term observed volatility of each asset. Table 8.1 lists the average standard deviation of the four since 1970 (TIPS are as of its 1998 inception).

Table 8.1   Average Standard Deviation of Equities, Treasuries, TIPS, and Commodities

Asset Class	Volatility Since 1970
Global Equities	15%
Long-Term Treasuries	11%
Long-Term TIPS	11%
Commodities (60% Industrial, 40% Gold)	15%

Source: Bloomberg.

Since we are seeking roughly equal upside from each asset class in its favored environment, we should attempt to achieve about the same weighted volatility from each market segment. A more technical way of saying the same thing is to strive for similar *risk exposure* across each asset class. The risk exposure comes from two sources:

1. Volatility
2. Allocation

The reason these two levers help control the risk exposure is that we are focused on the total impact on the portfolio of the individual asset class. If we allocate 1% to something, it doesn't matter much to the results of the total if it goes up or down, even if the volatility is high (say, 25%). The same goes for the volatility. If you allocate 25% to an asset class that only has 1% volatility and hardly moves around, then, when it is time for that asset to lead, it doesn't go up enough to keep the portfolio balanced from underperformance elsewhere.

In other words, if we allocate more capital to assets that are less volatile and less capital to assets that are more volatile, we can calibrate to an approximately equal risk exposure. Simplistically, we can take the volatility and multiply by the allocation for a data point to be used for comparison purposes. I will begin the balancing process by taking a simple first step. Using the earlier volatility, if we started with an equal 25% allocated to each asset class, we would end up with the imbalance presented in Table 8.2. This approach assumes equal *capital* allocation, as opposed to *risk* allocation, to each asset class.

Table 8.2   Equal *Capital* Allocation to Each Asset Class

Asset Class	Volatility		Allocation		Weighted Volatility
Global Equities	15%	×	25%	=	4%
Long-Term Treasuries	11%	×	25%	=	3%
Long-Term TIPS	11%	×	25%	=	3%
Commodities (60% Industrial, 40% Gold)	15%	×	25%	=	4%

Note: For illustration purposes only.

Notice that the weighted volatilities of Treasuries and TIPS are less than those of global equities and commodities. These asset classes are merely tools to gain exposure to various economic environments. As a result, this underrepresentation translates to underperformance during the economic environments during which Treasuries and TIPS are biased to outperform. Since both do better during falling growth, the portfolio of equal-weighted allocations to the four asset classes detailed in Table 8.2 would be biased to outperform during rising growth environments and underperform during falling growth. It isn't well-balanced from a growth perspective.

We can easily adjust our equally allocated portfolio to make it more balanced by increasing the percentage that goes to TIPS and Treasuries. You'll notice that equities and commodities are about 40% more volatile than TIPS and Treasuries (15% versus 11% standard deviation). Therefore, we need about 40% more allocation to the less risky asset classes to get them to equal risk exposure as summarized in Table 8.3.

Table 8.3   Equal *Risk* Allocation to Each Asset Class

Asset Class	Volatility		Allocation		Weighted Volatility
Global Equities	15%	×	25%	=	4%
Long-Term Treasuries	11%	×	35%	=	4%
Long-Term TIPS	11%	×	35%	=	4%
Commodities (60% Industrial, 40% Gold)	15%	×	25%	=	4%

Note: For illustration purposes only.

All four asset classes have similar weighted volatility, which indicates good balance. Note that adding up the allocations totals 120% (25% + 35% + 35% + 25%). This implies the need for a modest amount of leverage (20%) to achieve the desired balanced allocation. That is, $100 invested in the strategy provides $120 of total market exposure. As mentioned in the chapters on Treasuries and TIPS, those asset classes need some leverage to get them to equal return and risk as equities. The perspective shared here is another way of achieving the same objective.

The goal should be to minimize the cost of leverage to increase the expected return of the total portfolio net of any borrowing expenses. There is an elegant solution. Recall that, in the chapter about Treasuries, I presented the advantages of investing in Treasury futures instead of physical Treasury bonds to secure the exposure to this asset class.[1] One benefit of using futures is that no cash is needed to fund the exposure (recognizing the need to stay within margin requirements). In other words, we can gain the desired allocation to Treasuries without having to invest any cash. This is essentially another method to leverage the portfolio.

---

[1]Investing in futures involves risks and is not suitable for all investors. There are many factors that an investor should be aware of when trading futures, and investors should only engage in futures trading that is best suited to their financial condition and futures experience and that considers current market conditions. The use of derivative instruments, such as futures contracts, can lead to losses, which may be magnified by certain features of the derivatives.

More specifically, we would buy 35% of notional long-term Treasury exposure using futures. 85% of our cash would be used to purchase global equities (25%), commodities (25%), and long-term TIPS (35%). This leaves 15% left in cash that would be used as collateral for the Treasury futures contracts. The total notional exposure of all these holdings would make up our risk parity portfolio as summarized in Table 8.4.

Table 8.4 The Risk Parity Portfolio

Asset Class	Allocation
Global Equities	25%
Long-Term Treasuries	35%
Long-Term TIPS	35%
Commodities (60% Industrial, 40% Gold)	25%
Total Portfolio	**120%**

Note: For illustration purposes only.

RISK PARITY WITHOUT LEVERAGE OR WITH MORE LEVERAGE

The risk parity portfolio allocation described earlier is not universal. The concepts presented can be applied with various allocations and are completely applicable without leverage. The portfolio can also work with more leverage than detailed here. We can adjust the risk parity portfolio allocation up and down to increase or decrease the expected return and risk as needed. The proportion of risk to each asset class should not materially change in order to maintain balance. However, the total percentage allocated to each market segment can be ratcheted up or down.

For instance, instead of 25/35/35/25, we could completely eliminate the leverage in the portfolio by allocating 21/29/29/21 to the exact same asset classes. This allocation would roughly overweight TIPS and Treasuries (in terms of capital) by about the same as the levered version, resulting in a well-balanced allocation (in terms of risk). The difference, however, is that the percentages total 100%, implying no leverage at the portfolio level. Table 8.5 summarizes an unlevered risk parity portfolio allocation.

Table 8.5 An Unlevered Risk Parity Portfolio

Asset Class	Allocation
Global Equities	21%
Long-Term Treasuries	29%
Long-Term TIPS	29%
Commodities (60% Industrial, 40% Gold)	21%
Total Portfolio	**100%**

Note: For illustration purposes only.

The trade-off, of course, is a lower expected return with commensurately lower risk. The return-to-risk ratio is the same in both cases, but the level is different. The reason for the lower return and risk level can be expressed quite simply. If you invest $100 with an allocation of 21/29/29/21, then you are putting $21 in stocks, $29 in Treasuries, $29 in TIPS, and $21 in commodities. In the original risk parity portfolio, you would be investing about 20% more in each of the same assets. Obviously, $25 going into stocks versus $21 will yield higher potential returns and risk. In other words, in a year during which the risk parity portfolio earns 10% above cash, the unlevered version would return about 8% (20% less). The opposite is also true, which goes to the greater risk part of the trade-off: the unlevered portfolio would outperform the risk parity portfolio in a year during which it loses 10% by losing only about 8% (20% less).

Likewise, we can increase the leverage of the risk parity portfolio above 20% if we would like to target a higher level of return and risk over the long run. For example, the target allocation could be modified by increasing the allocation of each position by an additional 20%, which would result in 44% total portfolio leverage. Table 8.6 details this allocation.

Table 8.6 More Levered Risk Parity Portfolio

Asset Class	Allocation
Global Equities	30%
Long-Term Treasuries	42%
Long-Term TIPS	42%
Commodities (60% Industrial, 40% Gold)	30%
Total Portfolio	**144%**

Note: For illustration purposes only.

This more levered version of the risk parity portfolio will be more volatile than the original iteration. Of course, the expected return above cash will be about 20% greater as well. Another way to think of this is that, if you anticipate that the risk parity allocation will earn positive returns over your hold period (the longer the better), then a more levered version may make sense. The higher returns, of course, do not come without greater risk. What this means in practice, is you may sell at a downturn because of the pain associated with losses and therefore not benefit from the positive returns, even if they ultimately pan out over the long run. Therefore, the more levered allocation should be reserved for patient investors with a deep understanding of the risk parity concepts and those who are more focused on absolute returns as opposed to relative performance versus the stock market. Table 8.7 provides a summary of the three risk parity portfolio versions discussed for easy reference. I compare the returns, risk, and excess return-to-risk ratio (called the Sharpe Ratio) to global stocks and the traditional 60/40 allocation. All returns are since 1970.

Table 8.7   Summary of Three Risk Parity Portfolios with Different Leverage Amounts – January 1970 to March 2021

	Historical Total Return	Historical Excess Return	Historical Volatility	Sharpe Ratio
Risk Parity with No Leverage	9.8%	4.7%	9.0%	0.52
Risk Parity with 20% Leverage	10.7%	5.6%	10.8%	0.52
Risk Parity with 44% Leverage	11.7%	6.6%	12.9%	0.52
Global Equities	9.0%	4.0%	14.8%	0.27
60/40	8.6%	3.6%	9.5%	0.38

Note: For illustration purposes only.
Source: Bloomberg and Evoke Advisors analysis.

The math is relatively simple: the more leverage, the greater the return and risk, with an identical excess return-to-risk ratio across the board. All three risk parity mixes would have outperformed stocks over the past 51-plus years. The portfolio with no leverage also would have had less risk than the 60/40 mix. The 20% levered version would have exhibited slightly more risk than 60/40. The risk parity portfolio with the highest leverage amount would have handily beaten stocks and done it with less risk.

SUMMARY

I have now detailed our risk parity portfolio allocation. The emphasis should be on the conceptual framework presented rather than the precise allocations. My goal was to simplify the process to convey the logic behind building a well-balanced allocation. Keep in mind that introducing complexity doesn't necessarily improve results, given the art and science inherent in investing. In my experience, many inputs and assumptions can be imprecise. Thus, trying to fine tune the outcome can often lead to negative surprises. I strongly suggest emphasizing the core concepts in the pursuit to build balance, because greater confidence should lie in the timeless aspect of the overall framework than in the specifics.

CHAPTER NINE

Risk Parity Portfolio Historical Returns

From this point forward, I will be referring to the 20% levered version of the risk parity portfolio. The idea supporting this allocation is that it should offer the following:

1. Have a total return competitive with equities over the long run
2. Exhibit less risk than equities across three dimensions:
   a. Lower volatility
   b. More consistent returns over longer time frames (no lost decades)
   c. Significantly better downside protection

Since the strategy does not involve active management, we can easily go back in time to see if historical returns would have produced the results we would have expected through a variety of perspectives and different environments. We have a fixed allocation to each asset class, and each market segment has an index that can be back-tested through varying economic environments. This is unlike taking a more complex, active, rules-based approach that may be subject to data mining in an attempt to propose a strategy that may only be compelling looking backward. This is the main reason I continue to emphasize the concepts rather than the returns. A framework that is simple and sensible, using fundamental cause-effect relationships rather than a strategy that incorporates looser logical connections, is more robust and reliable looking forward.

Therefore, as I present the historical returns your focus should be on why it performed as it did during various economic environments and whether those outcomes are within reasonable expectations given the market conditions that transpired. By emphasizing the returns in this manner, you help reinforce the core concepts as if you actually lived through the past 50–100 years and viewed investment returns through the risk parity lens presented here. Approaching the problem from this perspective helps build confidence in its prospective returns and improves the likelihood of successful implementation in practice.

I will divide the historical returns into separate sections. First, I present results since 1998, which represents the longest common period for all of the underlying asset classes (this was the year in which long-term TIPS first began trading). I am also able to provide reliable data since 1970, because the other asset classes (equities, Treasuries, commodity producers, and gold) offer robust data sets since that time. I am able to proxy TIPS returns from 1970 to 1998 by allocating half of the target allocation each to Treasuries and gold. Although not a perfect substitute, these two asset classes combine to provide a reasonably correlated return to TIPS and are directionally similar.[1] Finally, we will review performance since 1926. This data is far more limited because, of the asset classes considered, only US equities (as opposed to global equities) and Treasuries have readily available and useful historical returns prior to 1970 (gold goes back much further but the price was fixed for many years). I include this imperfect data set as another reference point of the effectiveness of a risk parity approach even with a severely restricted menu of asset classes.

RETURNS SINCE 1998 (TIPS INCEPTION)

The fullest historical data set available starts in April 1998, which coincides with the inception of long-term TIPS in the United States. Table 9.1 provides the historical returns and volatility of the risk parity portfolio from April 1998 until March 2021 (rebalanced monthly). I compare returns to global equities and a conventional 60/40 portfolio.

---

[1]Use of a different proxy and a different set of assumptions and methodologies for TIPS will likely yield different results, and in some cases those differences may be material.

Table 9.1   Risk Parity Portfolio versus Global Equities and 60/40 – April 1998 to March 2021

Portfolio	Average Total Return	Average Excess Return	Average Volatility
Risk Parity	9.2%	7.1%	10.2%
Global Equities	6.2%	4.1%	15.6%
60/40	6.0%	3.9%	9.4%

Source: Bloomberg.

The risk parity portfolio has outpaced global equities and 60/40 by about 3% per annum over the past 23 years with about two-thirds of the risk of stocks and comparable volatility as 60/40 (which is consistent with my long-term expectations). For additional insight into performance during various periods, Table 9.2 breaks down the returns by decade.

Table 9.2   Risk Parity Portfolio versus Global Equities and 60/40 – by Decade*

Portfolio	2010s	2000s
Risk Parity	8.1%	10.5%
Global Equities	9.5%	–0.2%
60/40	7.4%	2.7%

* Total annualized returns listed. As a point of reference, cash returned 0.6% per year in the 2010s and 3.0% in the 2000s.
Source: Bloomberg.

Risk parity has delivered more consistent returns than both global equities and the conventional 60/40 mix when examined through this perspective. During the decade of the 2010s equities outperformed by 1.4% per annum but trailed by 10.7% per year during the 2000s. 60/40, which is more balanced than a 100% equity allocation, didn't go up as much in the recent decade but held up better during the negative decade for stocks. Still, risk parity beat 60/40 in each decade.

More noticeably, equities actually lost money during that 10-year stretch resulting in the famed "lost decade." Cash earned an annualized 0.6% in the 2010s and 3.0% during the 2000s. Subtracting the total returns from the cash returns reveals a very interesting discovery. *The risk parity portfolio actually achieved the exact same excess return in both decades (7.5%).* This occurred despite a markedly different economic environment as evidenced by the widely diverging equity market returns, which were strongly positive during the recent decade and negative the decade prior.

Zooming in a little further, Table 9.3 summarizes the total returns of the risk parity portfolio, global equities, and 60/40 by full calendar year since 1999 (the first full year since mid-1998).

Table 9.3   Risk Parity Portfolio versus Global Equities and 60/40 – by Calendar Year

Year	Risk Parity	Global Equities	60/40	Year	Risk Parity	Global Equities	60/40
1999	9.1%	24.9%	14.1%	2010	17.2%	11.8%	10.2%
2000	7.0%	–13.2%	–3.8%	2011	16.7%	–5.5%	0.0%
2001	1.7%	–16.8%	–7.0%	2012	12.6%	15.8%	11.3%
2002	11.3%	–19.9%	–8.4%	2013	–10.2%	26.7%	14.5%
2003	22.9%	33.1%	20.9%	2014	15.1%	4.9%	5.4%
2004	15.6%	14.7%	10.5%	2015	–8.7%	–0.9%	–0.1%
2005	13.6%	9.5%	6.7%	2016	11.9%	7.5%	5.7%
2006	11.6%	20.1%	13.6%	2017	17.0%	22.4%	14.5%
2007	21.5%	9.0%	8.3%	2018	–7.1%	–8.7%	–5.1%
2008	–12.8%	–40.7%	–24.7%	2019	23.0%	27.7%	20.0%
2009	17.5%	30.0%	20.4%	2020	23.7%	15.9%	13.3%

Source: Bloomberg.

Observing the data from an absolute return standpoint, the risk parity portfolio suffered fewer negative years than global equities (four versus seven) and 60/40 (four versus six). Most impressively, it generally offered stronger downside protection during the worst environments like 2000–2002 (positive each year versus double-digit losses for global stocks each year) and 2008 (–13% versus –41%). Risk parity also outpaced 60/40 during each of these major downturns. In fact, the risk parity mix produced a net *positive* cumulative return over these four equity-bear-market years – which are the worst that we've experienced for many decades – during which 66% of value vanished from the stock market and 38% from 60/40!

Another notable point is that the risk parity portfolio can be volatile. Most of the historical returns, like equities, have been in the double digits. That said, the odds of a material decline are much lower than stocks, because of the balance inherent in the allocation. This is clearly evident by examining the long-term returns by calendar year. The types of environments that typically cause big losses in equities are also the same periods that tend to be favorable for other asset classes. To illustrate this point, I highlight in Table 9.4 the various asset-class total returns during the four calendar years since 1998 when equities suffered a major setback.

Table 9.4   Asset-Class Returns During Major Equity Down Years

Asset Class	2000	2001	2002	2008
Global Equities	–13.2%	–16.8%	–19.9%	–40.7%
Long Treasuries	20.3%	4.2%	16.8%	24.0%
Long TIPS	17.9%	9.8%	21.2%	0.4%
60/40 Commodities/Gold	–1.4%	–0.7%	10.3%	–24.9%
Gold	–5.5%	2.5%	24.8%	5.8%
Commodities	1.4%	–2.8%	0.6%	–45.3%
Risk Parity	**7.0%**	**1.7%**	**11.3%**	**–12.8%**

Source: Bloomberg.

Treasuries have demonstrated the clearest hedge against an equity market downturn since 1998, delivering bull market returns just when diversification was most needed. TIPS have also shown strong diversification benefits during these four market downturns. As referenced in earlier chapters, the reason these results make sense is that the stock market underwent a major hit as growth unexpectedly collapsed. From 2000 to 2002, the dot-com bubble burst caused the decline, whereas the 2008 drop resulted from an enormous housing and credit crisis. As expected, interest rates fell in response to the plunge in economic activity. Predictably, Treasuries and TIPS rallied as they are fundamentally structured to do when rates fall. Note that I am not at all suggesting I knew these outcomes would occur in advance. The cause–effect relationship between an economic collapse and interest rates is the point of emphasis as opposed to the accurate timing of these events in advance.

As I expand our data set to include the 1970s, you will see that equities may also underperform during rising inflationary periods. Since interest rates may also rise during these environments, Treasuries may not provide the same protection as we've witnessed during the past two decades when shifts in inflation were less of a factor. Inflation hedges like TIPS, commodities, and gold are better positioned to help the total portfolio weather equity storms resulting from upside inflation surprises.

Zooming out a little, Table 9.5 details the total return of the five asset classes over the full period from April 1998 to March 2021.

Table 9.5   Asset-Class Returns – April 1998 to March 2021

Asset Class	Average Total Return	Average Excess Return	Average Volatility
Global Equities	6.2%	4.1%	15.6%
Long Treasuries	6.5%	4.5%	12.3%
Long TIPS	7.2%	5.2%	10.5%
60/40 Commodities/Gold	9.2%	7.1%	16.1%
Gold	*7.8%*	*5.7%*	*16.5%*
Commodity Producers	*9.1%*	*7.0%*	*20.9%*
Risk Parity	**9.2%**	**7.1%**	**10.2%**

Source: Bloomberg.

Two observations stand out from this table of returns. First, equities were the worst-performing asset class over the full term. This is largely due to the lost decade, which doesn't happen very often but occurred over our measurement period. This may surprise investors who strongly believe that equities are the best-performing asset class for the long run. In reality, the long run may be much longer than many may imagine. In this case, 23 years is not long enough for stocks to win.

Also, it is common to compare equities to other asset classes that are less risky than equities. Since they are less risky, it makes sense that they would underperform equities over the long run. The comparison is not apples-to-apples. With the risk parity portfolio, we seek to structure each asset class to deliver comparable returns over the long run because they have similar risk. In this respect, you'll note that the historical risk of Treasuries and TIPS since 1998 is less than that of equities (even though the returns over this time frame were superior). Returns will fluctuate over time, but the risk levels are more stable over long stretches. This is why I overweight TIPS and Treasuries (35% each) versus equities and commodities (25% each). The return contribution from each of the asset classes over the very long run is designed to be comparable. Therefore, TIPS and Treasuries do not have to perform as well as they have since 1998 to provide similar upside to the portfolio looking forward. They are expected to earn 40% less than stocks (excess returns) with about 40% less risk.

Second, a distinct rebalancing benefit is apparent from a high-level analysis of the 23-year data. *The risk parity portfolio's average return over the full term is higher than the average return of any of the underlying asset classes!* Moreover, the average risk or volatility is lower than any single asset class. The lower risk makes sense because of the diversification benefits associated with superior balance. Most investors already appreciate the advantage of reduced risk that comes from prudent diversification. However, in my experience there is significant underappreciation of the boost in returns that can come from strong diversification. This is particularly true when the various investments have low correlation to one another *and* are individually volatile. This is such an important, undervalued point that I devote Chapter 11 to it.

RETURNS SINCE 1970

While the live track record of US TIPS began in 1998, all the other asset classes have available return histories that began several decades earlier. In the chapter on TIPS, I described the potential to proxy TIPS with a 50/50 allocation to Treasuries and gold. TIPS are biased to outperform during falling growth and rising inflation environments. Treasuries provide the downside growth protection while gold offers upside during periods driven by rising inflation. Since we don't have actual TIPS returns prior to 1998, we can use Treasuries and gold to provide some longer-term historical perspective. To test the similarities between these two allocations, I compared the returns of TIPS to a 50/50 Treasury/gold allocation from April 1998 to March 2021 (the live track record of TIPS). The average return was 7.2% for TIPS and 7.5% for the 50/50 allocation. Volatility was also comparable at 10.5% TIPS and 10.9% Treasuries/gold. The correlation of monthly returns between the two return streams came in at 0.66 over the 23 years. They are not perfect substitutes but are relatively close and sufficient to allow us to extend our return series over a longer period to demonstrate the general performance pattern over varying economic environments.[2] My main goal was to capture the inflationary 1970s in our data set since inflation has been on a general downtrend since then and may pick up again sometime in the future.

In Table 9.6, I show the historical returns of the risk parity portfolio substituting in the 50/50 Treasury/gold allocation for TIPS from 1970 to April 1998. In practice, this results in an increased allocation of 17.5% each to Treasuries and gold on top of the existing 35% and 10% holdings, respectively, for the period prior to TIPS' inception in April 1998. I compare the results to global equities and 60/40 as I did before.

Table 9.6   Risk Parity Portfolio versus Global Equities and 60/40 – January 1970 to March 2021

Portfolio	Average Total Return	Average Excess Return	Average Volatility
Risk Parity with TIPS substitute prior to 1998	10.7%	5.6%	10.8%
Global Equities	9.0%	4.0%	14.8%
60/40	8.6%	3.6%	9.5%

Source: Bloomberg.

Risk parity beat global equities by 1.7% per year over the past 51-plus years with about two-thirds the risk! The volatility difference between risk parity and global equities is comparable to the results we saw in the period since 1998. The return difference, although still impressive at 1.7% per year over 51-plus years, is less than it has been since 1998. This reflects the inclusion of the historic equity bull market of the 1980s and 1990s in our data set. Even with one of the greatest bull markets on record, risk parity still outperformed while taking less risk. Results since 1970 are also impressive in comparison to 60/40 as they have been since 1998.

Table 9.7 compares total returns by each over the past five decades.

[2]Use of a different proxy and a different set of assumptions and methodologies for TIPS will likely yield different results, and in some cases those differences may be material.

Table 9.7   Risk Parity Portfolio versus Global Equities and 60/40 – by Decade*

Portfolio	2010s	2000s	1990s	1980s	1970s
Risk Parity	8.1%	10.5%	8.1%	11.6%	15.1%
Global Equities	9.5%	–0.2%	11.4%	18.8%	5.7%
60/40	7.4%	2.7%	10.2%	16.5%	6.4%

* Total annualized returns listed. As a point of reference, cash returned 0.6% per year in the 2010s, 3.0% in the 2000s, 5.3% in the 1990s, 10.0% in the 1980s, 6.3% in the 1970s.
Source: Bloomberg.

Note that global equities underperformed cash in two of the five decades (2000s and 1970s). In the other three decades returns were very strong and ahead of the risk parity portfolio. However, risk parity ended up achieving superior returns over the entire 51-plus years not only with lower volatility, but perhaps more important, with greater consistency. There were no lost decades. Even the traditional 60/40 portfolio suffered through two bad decades – the 2000s, when it trailed cash, and the 1970s, when it barely kept pace with cash. These results are predictable given the economic outcomes during those periods. Growth significantly fell short of expectations in the 2000s, and inflation materially outpaced what had been discounted during the 1970s. Both economic environments pose headwinds for equities, which is why they severely underperformed those two decades.

To gain a clearer picture of how the stability of risk parity came about, I dive into the various asset-class total returns by decade in Table 9.8. I also include the 51-plus-year average return and risk by asset class as another point of reference.

Table 9.8   Asset-Class Returns by Decade*

Asset Class	2010s	2000s	1990s	1980s	1970s	51-plus Years	Volatility
Global Equities	9.5%	–0.2%	11.4%	18.8%	5.7%	9.0%	14.8%
Long Treasuries	7.0%	7.6%	8.6%	12.8%	5.6%	8.1%	10.6%
Long TIPS	5.9%	9.4%	–	–	–	7.2%**	10.5%**
50/50 Treasuries/Gold	5.5%	11.3%	2.8%	5.9%	19.1%	8.7%	11.4%
60/40 Commodities/Gold	3.6%	15.1%	6.8%	7.9%	20.7%	10.7%	15.2%
Gold	*3.3%*	*14.3%*	*–3.3%*	*–2.4%*	*30.7%*	*7.9%*	*19.2%*
Commodity Producers	*3.0%*	*14.6%*	*13.1%*	*14.1%*	*12.6%*	*11.4%*	*18.8%*
Risk Parity	**8.1%**	**10.5%**	**8.1%**	**11.6%**	**15.1%**	**10.7%**	**10.8%**

* Total annualized returns listed. As a point of reference, cash returned 0.6% per year in the 2010s, 3.0% in the 2000s, 5.3% in the 1990s, 10.0% in the 1980s, 6.3% in the 1970s. The average return of cash over the full 51-plus years was 4.9%.
** TIPS returns/risk since April 1998. Cash earned 1.9% and global equities 6.2% during this time frame.
Source: Bloomberg.

Reviewing the wide dispersion of returns by asset class over the same five decades provides useful insight. This view helps to show how the portfolio and the different asset classes performed during very different times. We can analyze results during the inflationary 1970s when interest rates rose to midteens. On a total return basis, that environment actually marked the best decade for the risk parity portfolio. While stocks and Treasuries underperformed cash for 10 years, the inflation-hedged assets of gold and commodities surged in value. TIPS didn't exist at the time but would have likely enjoyed a tailwind as the economic environment of generally rising inflation and falling growth (stagflation) favored that asset class, as can be roughly proxied by the exceptional performance of the 50/50 Treasury/gold allocation.

The 1980s and 1990s were dominated by falling inflation, improving growth, and gradually declining interest rates from historic highs. This was an economic climate nearly the opposite of the prior decade. The best asset in the 1970s, gold, proceeded to lose money over the ensuing 20 years while equities and Treasuries enjoyed their two best decades (as would be anticipated given the environment that transpired).

Then we had the lost decade for equities during the 2000s when commodities were the best assets to own up until the Global Financial Crisis. I started in the industry just before this decade and clearly recall few market analysts anticipating one of the worst decades for stocks as we turned the calendars to the new millennium after the greatest bull market in history. The downside growth assets performed strongly as TIPS and gold enjoyed strong returns amid two major economic downturns to significantly outpace stocks over the 10 years. Commodities also enjoyed a bull market during the 2000s on the heels of booming demand from emerging economies that experienced rising growth even though the United States did not.

The most recent decade of the 2010s delivered an environment that is the mirror image of the prior decade with equities outperforming everything else and commodities finishing in last place. This result makes sense since growth significantly outperformed expectations following the lost decade and proved to be the main driver of asset-class returns. Because of falling inflation, commodities, gold, and TIPS trailed equities and Treasuries during the decade.

With the common recency bias to which most investors are prone, few market participants are overly excited about commodities today. Even though commodity producer equities have outperformed global stocks by over 2% per year over the past 51-plus years, the fresh memory of poor results over a perceived long stretch can dissuade investors from buying.

The other notable point about the data in Table 9.8 is that the risk parity portfolio's returns since 1970 are near the top when compared to the underlying holdings (only behind commodity producers). Again, this comes from the benefits of prudent diversification across a diverse set of individually risky asset classes biased to outperform in varying economic climates and the rebalancing boost that accrues over time (that will be covered shortly).

The final observation from this long-term data set that I'd like you to note is the volatility of the various asset classes. Global equities and the combined commodity mix have had about 15% volatility over the full period. Treasuries and TIPS, since their inceptions, have had standard deviations of about 11%. In the previous chapter, I used these long-term figures to determine the weighting to each asset class.

The other major objective of a balanced asset allocation is to better protect during major bear markets. An equity bear market is typically defined as a peak to trough loss of around 20%. Since 1970, there have been nine periods during which global stocks declined by about this much. Table 9.9 compares the total returns of the risk parity portfolio to global equities over these peak-to-trough periods.

Table 9.9   Risk Parity During Historical Bear Markets

Bear Market	Peak-to-Trough	Global Equities	Risk Parity
Continuation of late 1960s bear market	12/69–6/70	−19.1%	−7.9%
Bretton Woods	3/73–9/74	−41.1%	−2.8%
Fed tightening	11/80–7/82	−19.3%	−23.4%
Black Monday	8/87–11/87	−20.5%	−6.4%
Gulf War	12/89–/90	−24.3%	−6.5%
Dot-Com bust	3/00–9/02	−46.8%	10.3%
Global financial crisis	10/07–2/09	−54.0%	−19.9%
Eurozone crisis	4/11–9/11	−19.6%	4.1%
Global pandemic	12/19–3/20	−21.1%	−0.8%
Average		**−29.5%**	**−5.9%**

* I include a few instances when the equity drop on a monthly basis was slightly less than 20% to capture periods that were greater than 20% when considering intra-month peak-to-trough drawdowns. *Source:* Bloomberg.

Note that risk parity outperformed on the downside in eight out of nine bear markets and posted an average decline of just −5.9% versus −29.5% for global equities. There has been a clear advantage for being better diversified in the worst equity markets.

It is also important to recognize that the risk parity portfolio will experience its own bear markets that will likely be unrelated to an equity market downturn. I examined all the periods during which the risk parity portfolio lost more than 20% from its peak to trough since 1970. Table 9.10 summarizes the results of my findings of the two occasions.

Table 9.10   Risk Parity Bear Markets

Bear Market	Peak-to-Trough	Global Equities	Risk Parity
Fed tightening	6/80–6/82	–5.2%	–26.2%
Global Financial Crisis	2/08–2/09	–47.1%	–23.9%
Average		**–26.1%**	**–25.0%**

Source: Bloomberg.

Only twice since 1970 has the risk parity portfolio suffered a drawdown of at least 20%. Note that during the first quarter of 2020 the risk parity portfolio was only down about 1% (as shown in Table 9.9), but intramonth it did approach a decline from peak-to-trough close to 20% as global equities plummeted by 35% over a five-week period. In Chapter 13 I will further explain the underperformance versus equities during the Fed tightening period of the early 1980s, because this is an important economic environment during which risk parity may underperform.

I end this section by listing the calendar year total returns of the risk parity portfolio, global equities, and 60/40 from 1970 to 2020. Returns since 1998 will match those listed in Table 9.3. The results are shown in Table 9.11.

Table 9.11   Risk Parity Portfolio versus Global Equities and 60/40 – by Calendar Year

Year	Risk Parity	Global Equities	60/40	Year	Risk Parity	Global Equities	60/40
1970	9.6%	–3.1%	4.7%	1996	3.0%	13.5%	9.5%
1971	22.6%	18.4%	14.7%	1997	3.3%	15.8%	13.5%
1972	25.2%	22.5%	15.3%	1998	7.2%	24.3%	18.5%
1973	9.3%	–15.2%	–7.4%	1999	9.1%	24.9%	14.1%
1974	6.6%	–25.5%	–13.8%	2000	7.0%	–13.2%	–3.8%
1975	8.0%	32.8%	22.7%	2001	1.7%	–16.8%	–7.0%
1976	15.3%	13.4%	13.8%	2002	11.3%	–19.9%	–8.4%
1977	5.2%	0.7%	1.6%	2003	22.9%	33.1%	20.9%
1978	15.7%	16.5%	10.4%	2004	15.6%	14.7%	10.5%
1979	36.8%	11.0%	7.3%	2005	13.6%	9.5%	6.7%
1980	14.6%	25.7%	16.5%	2006	11.6%	20.1%	13.6%
1981	–16.4%	–4.8%	–0.4%	2007	21.5%	9.0%	8.3%
1982	23.3%	9.7%	18.6%	2008	–12.8%	–40.7%	–24.7%
1983	4.0%	21.9%	16.4%	2009	17.5%	30.0%	20.4%
1984	0.5%	4.7%	9.0%	2010	17.2%	11.8%	10.2%
1985	29.0%	40.6%	32.9%	2011	16.7%	–5.5%	0.0%
1986	30.4%	41.9%	30.8%	2012	12.6%	15.8%	11.3%
1987	11.6%	16.2%	11.6%	2013	–10.2%	26.7%	14.5%
1988	7.6%	23.3%	17.1%	2014	15.1%	4.9%	5.4%
1989	20.5%	16.6%	16.0%	2015	–8.7%	–0.9%	–0.1%
1990	–3.9%	–17.0%	–7.0%	2016	11.9%	7.5%	5.7%
1991	20.1%	18.3%	17.6%	2017	17.0%	22.4%	14.5%
1992	2.9%	–5.2%	–0.3%	2018	–7.1%	–8.7%	–5.1%
1993	25.0%	22.5%	17.4%	2019	23.0%	27.7%	20.0%
1994	–3.3%	5.1%	1.9%	2020	23.7%	15.9%	13.3%
1995	22.1%	20.7%	20.0%	**Average**	**10.7%**	**9.0%**	**8.6%**

Source: Bloomberg.

The past 51-plus years have demonstrated that the risk parity portfolio has exhibited stronger downside protection with only 7 down years against 13 for global stocks and 11 for 60/40. In addition, the risk parity portfolio only lost 10% or more three times since 1970: 1981 (–16%), 2008 (–13%), and 2013 (–10%).

It is one thing to say you can live with the sporadic big losses because you know it pays off over the long run. But it is another to learn that you could have avoided the pain and earned more for the full period. Conventional wisdom states that higher risk is rewarded with greater returns over time. What is rarely appreciated is that a properly diversified portfolio can allow for *better returns with less risk*. This is why diversification is often considered the one "free lunch" in investing. You get more without giving up anything. The main purpose of this book is to provide the framework to better appreciate a way to build a more efficient asset allocation using simple asset classes and a basic timeless approach.

Figure 9.1 sums it all up in one picture. If you would have invested $1 in each strategy in January 1970 and checked your account in March 2021, you would have $182 with the risk parity portfolio, $84 with equities, and $69 with 60/40 (rebalanced monthly).

Figure 9.1 $1 Invested in Risk Parity, Equities, and 60/40 – January 1970 to March 2021

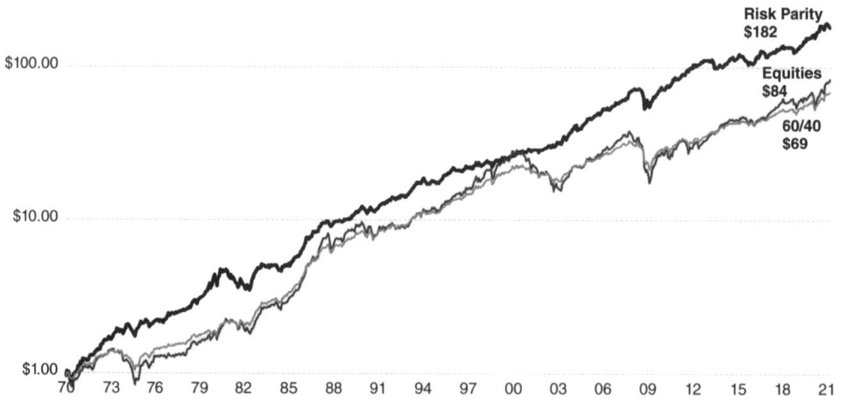

Note: Hypothetical returns provided for illustrative purposes only.

RETURNS SINCE 1926

Treasuries and US equities have longer, reliable, and widely available data series prior to 1970. These two asset classes completely miss balancing against the rising inflation economic environment (since both are biased to underperform during rising inflation), but we can look at returns going back to 1926 as some indication of how a balanced mix of equities and Treasuries would have performed. Since we are missing valuable inflation hedges, this analysis is less relevant than the 1970 to 2021 period (which, in turn, is less informative than the performance of the fully balanced mix since 1998). Given the limited usefulness of data since 1926, I will focus my attention in this section on conveying two key points that support the foundation upon which risk parity is based:

1. By using the risk parity framework, investors could have earned a comparable return from Treasuries (using leverage) as equities over the past 95 years (from 1926 to 2021).
2. Owning both equities and Treasuries would have produced a more stable return than either asset class individually.

Table 9.12 details the historical returns and risk of the stock market (US equities only until 1970; global stocks thereafter) and long-term Treasuries from January 1926 to March 2021.

Table 9.12   Equities and Unlevered Treasuries – January 1926 to March 2021*

	Average Total Return	Average Excess Return	Average Volatility
Equities	8.9%	5.3%	18.5%
Unlevered Treasuries	5.9%	2.3%	10.5%

* Note that cash earned 3.5% per year over this period.
Source: Bloomberg.

We've all heard the long-held mantra that stocks beat bonds over the long run. The data in Table 9.12 certainly backs this conclusion. However, the reason stocks outperform over the long run is simply because they are far riskier than Treasuries. If we match the risk of Treasuries to that of equities, then the returns are unsurprisingly comparable over nearly a century. Note that the ratio of excess return above cash and volatility are relatively close. Equities are 0.28, whereas Treasuries are 0.22. This means equities have earned about 0.28 units of excess return per unit of risk, whereas Treasuries slightly trail from an efficiency standpoint at 0.22. Over time, these figures tend to be closely aligned, although they can deviate slightly depending on the starting and ending point of the measurement period. For example, if we look at the same data at the end of 2008, the ratio is 0.23 for stocks and 0.20 for Treasuries over the 80-plus-year period.

When the ratios are about the same, then we can simply lever up the lower risk asset class to a similar volatility to produce a comparable long-term return. The simplified math using the average volatility of each asset class since 1926 would cause us to own roughly 1.75 times as much in Treasuries as equities. Therefore, if we were to pick a single asset class over the near 100-year period, investing in stocks or levered Treasuries would have yielded similar returns. Stocks earned about 9% per year. We can easily lever Treasuries by investing in futures contracts as described in Chapter 4. If we had targeted a notional exposure of about 1.75 times or 175%, then the historical return since 1926 would have been approximately 8% per annum. Had we applied the same basic methodology at the end of 2008, the returns for the two asset classes would have been an identical 8% over 80 years.

The other critical point is that thoughtful diversification can help reduce risk and increase returns over the long run. Using our stock and Treasury data series since 1926, we can observe these results. Table 9.13 lists the returns and risk of each asset class again but also includes a portfolio that allocated 50% of the *risk* to each (rebalanced monthly for ease). The capital allocation for this portfolio would be 50% equities and 88% Treasuries, suggesting 38% of total portfolio leverage.

Table 9.13   Equities, Treasuries, and 50/50 Mix – January 1926 to March 2021*

	Average Total Return	Average Excess Return	Average Volatility
Equities	8.9%	5.3%	18.5%
Treasuries	5.9%	2.3%	10.5%
50/50 Mix	8.5%	4.9%	12.0%

* Note that cash earned 3.5% per year over this period.
Source: Bloomberg.

The returns of the equal *risk-weighted* portfolio are only slightly below equities over nearly 100 years, and the risk is materially lower (12.0% versus 18.5%). In Table 9.14, I compare results by decade to help paint the picture of greater stability. The Great Depression years of the 1930s stand out in this regard.

Table 9.14   Equities, Treasuries, and 50/50 Risk Balanced Mix – by Decade*

Asset Class	1960s	1950s	1940s	1930s
Equities	7.8%	19.3%	9.5%	−3.4%
Treasuries	−1.3%	−2.2%	6.0%	9.1%
50/50 Mix	3.8%	8.7%	7.8%	3.9%

* Total annualized returns listed. As a point of reference, cash returned 3.9% per year in the 1960s, 1.9% in the 1950s, 0.4% in the 1940s, 0.6% in the 1930s.
Source: Bloomberg.

The 50/50 risk balanced mix did not experience a lost decade even during the 1930s, when it turned in a respectable 3.9% annual average, outperforming the stock market by over 7% per annum. During the 1960s, the 50/50 portfolio did not do as well because of rising inflation pressures in the second half of the decade. Clearly, owning a large allocation to inflation hedges would have meaningfully improved total returns over the full period.

Finally, I review total returns through equity bear markets of 20% or greater drawdowns from peak-to-trough in Table 9.15. There were seven such events before 1970.

Table 9.15 Risk Balanced Mix during Equity Bear Markets pre-1970

Peak-to-Trough	Global Equities	50/50 Risk-Balanced Mix
8/29–6/32	–86.0%	–55.8%
2/37–3/38	–49.7%	–27.7%
4/40–5/40	–24.0%	–14.6%
7/41–4/42	–22.7%	–11.3%
5/46–5/47	–21.2%	–10.4%
12/61–6/62	–22.2%	–9.0%
1/66–8/66	–28.8%	–24.4%
Average	**–36.4%**	**–21.9%**

Source: Bloomberg.

The 50/50 risk-balanced allocation between equities and Treasuries held up better in every bear market, including the worst one ever in the United States during the Great Depression. Obviously, the downside protection should not be expected to be as robust as with the full risk parity portfolio since there are several critical missing components. However, even with a limited menu of choices, a more balanced allocation can achieve comparable long-term returns with less volatility, more consistent returns by environment and, as demonstrated earlier, better downside protection during the most severe market downturns.

SUMMARY

The purpose of this chapter is to bring together all the concepts presented to this point by studying the long-term return history of the risk parity portfolio. Through the historical data, I am able to quantitatively demonstrate the advantages of a balanced allocation to support the logical framework behind the strategy. From a risk standpoint, the risk parity portfolio is more like 60/40. However, risk parity has outperformed equities over all time frames measured. Such a combination was achieved with a simple well-balanced asset allocation that is intuitive despite being unconventional.

With a thorough analysis of the historical returns of the various asset classes and the risk parity portfolio, I believe I have been able to show compelling evidence over extremely long periods of time. The analysis since 1998 is the most thorough, but performance since 1970 is exceptionally robust. This measurement period covers five very different decades to provide insight into the long-term stability of the approach through completely different economic environments. By including limited data that goes back to just before the Great Depression, we are able to gain additional understanding about the benefits of diversification during some of the darkest times in market history.

In Chapter 10, we will shift our focus from looking backward at historical returns to considering what the future economic environment may look like. Clearly, the future will be different from the past in ways we won't know until after the fact. This is particularly evident today with the wide range of potential economic outcomes looking forward. Studying how the risk parity portfolio has withstood the test of time for the past century gives us greater confidence in its prospective viability. We obviously won't know the final results until time passes, but by analyzing historical returns we should feel better about the potential to achieve our main objectives of earning equity-like returns with less risk.

CHAPTER TEN

The Timeliness
of Risk Parity

There is an old saying, "May you live in interesting times." Whether this expression implies a blessing or a curse, it was unquestionably applicable when I wrote this book in 2021. The key headlines are nothing short of extraordinary. Interest rates in the United States and throughout much of the world are at or, in many cases, below 0%. This has never happened before. The United States is running the largest non-wartime budget deficit on record by an astounding margin, causing our national debt to balloon out of control. To finance the increased spending, major central banks continue to engage in quantitative easing on an unprecedented scale with no signs of slowing. Populism is clearly on the rise as a growing number of citizens are expressing anger at the establishment and demanding change. To top it all off, COVID-19 – a microscopic global enemy the likes of which none of us have seen in our lifetimes – wreaked havoc across the planet by derailing economies and inflicting a worldwide healthcare emergency. Certainly, the state of the global economy is not all negative as rapid technological innovation continues to improve productivity and effective vaccines were rolled out at a record pace. The net of the backdrop, however, is undoubtedly concerning.

Making money when markets rally is relatively easy, but the hardest part about investing – and the key to long-term success – is to protect principal during severe market downturns and avoid catastrophic losses. Therefore, from a big picture perspective, maintaining a well-balanced portfolio is prudent *all the time*. However, in the unique environment in which we currently live, the importance of being balanced is absolutely paramount.

You may be familiar with some of these headlines, but in this chapter-I will walk through the mechanics of why balance is so critical today. A well-informed appreciation of the main forces that drive economies and markets is required to fully grasp the heightened risks that lie ahead. I begin with a description of the role of the central bank in managing the economy and the tools it has at its disposal. I then shift to analyzing the major headwinds and tailwinds that are at play, including the political uncertainty that can influence markets and economies. The conclusion will explain why investing in a well-balanced allocation today is imperative because of the unusually wide range of potential economic outcomes and the greater risk of extreme results when looking ahead.

THE CENTRAL BANK

I learned the main concepts described in this chapter from Bridgewater Associates, a firm at the forefront of economic and investment research. Ray Dalio, Bob Prince, Greg Jensen and their team have been developing and refining their understanding of the economic machine over the past four decades. I have absorbed tremendous knowledge from Bridgewater over the years, but perhaps their most foundational insight is their understanding of the mechanics of the economic machine. I strongly urge you to visit their website www.economicprinciples.com and watch the 30-minute video "How the Economic Machine Works."

In many ways, the central bank can be viewed as the nation's doctor while the economy is the patient. Most of the time, the economy is capable of self-adjusting to bumps and bruises without the need for major intervention. It may occasionally fall ill and seek medical assistance, and the doctor prescribes the typical medicine for the sickness. Every now and then the patient may suffer a major ailment and require emergency medical attention, which requires the doctor to dig deeper into his or her medical toolkit. Should the patient suffer a catastrophic decline in health, then the doctor would be called to use any and all measures within its power to save the patient.

Economies routinely oscillate through expansions and contractions with occasional major booms and painful busts. The normal business cycle, as this is commonly known, is part of the process of how economies regularly operate. The central bank's fundamental responsibility is to smooth out fluctuations of these economic cycles by serving as a counterforce utilizing their unique toolkit. The highest priority is to minimize the risk of extreme environments – such as depression or hyperinflation – and limit collateral economic damage (including high levels of unemployment). Should severely adverse environments transpire, then it is the central bank that can serve as the last resort to pull the economy back into the safe zone. For these reasons, the central bank serves as a major player in economic outcomes, which by and large are the key influence on the shape of markets.

The health of the economy is typically measured in terms of economic growth and price stability (or inflation). The Fed does not want the economy to weaken too much, because reduced spending feeds into falling incomes, which begets more spending cuts by households and corporations, resulting in a negative feedback loop. We saw this in 2008 and again in early 2020. The Fed also does not want prices to rise too rapidly. If there is too much money chasing too few goods, services, and financial assets, then upward pressure can be exerted on prices, which can be harmful to an economy if it goes too far. The 1970s provided a good example of the problems high inflation can present, including elevated unemployment and general economic stagnation. Perhaps most important, the Fed wishes to avoid deflation and depression, which can be very difficult to reverse. When general prices commence on a downward path, then consumers tend to wait for prices to fall before buying, which creates a negative feedback loop of reduced spending. This feedback loop can prove very difficult to break. Japan has been suffering through a deflationary environment since the 1990s, despite years of expansionary monetary and fiscal policy. In short, the Fed seeks to achieve a goldilocks economy: moderate growth and low inflation – not too hot, not too cold, but just right.

The Fed's Main Policy Tool: Interest Rates

The Fed is equipped with a few powerful tools to successfully manage the economy. The main policy tool at the Fed's disposal is the ability to control short-term interest rates. This tool works perfectly well nearly all the time. Only the Fed has the privilege of managing the Fed Funds rate, which is the interest rate banks use to lend to the real economy. The Fed's autonomy is intentionally separated from other branches of government to help it maintain the integrity of its dual mandate: manage economic growth and inflation for the benefit of the economy without political influences.

Whenever growth weakens or inflation is too low, the Fed can stimulate the economy by employing its main tool and lowering short-term interest rates. Lower rates stimulate borrowing since the cost of debt is reduced. Think of a typical mortgage as an example. The prevailing interest rate on financing your home is heavily influenced by the interest rate set by the Fed. When the Fed reduces interest rates, there is typically a reduction in the interest rate charged on mortgages since the cost of capital for banks is lower. You can buy a more expensive home when mortgage rates are 4% (as they are today) than when they sit at 14% (as was the case in the 1980s) since the monthly mortgage payments would be considerably lower. Moreover, whenever rates drop, you have the opportunity to refinance your existing mortgage to reduce your monthly payment for the same loan amount and the same house. This puts extra money in your pocket that can be spent elsewhere. Take this example and apply it across a wide range of lending markets and multiply by millions of citizens. You can imagine the overall impact and potency that comes with controlling interest rates as more borrowing injects capital into the economy and/or markets, which provides the needed boost to improve growth or increase inflation from depressed levels, as increased spending bids up prices. In short, this medicine is extremely powerful and can address the vast majority of health concerns for our patient.

The reverse also works effectively. When growth is too strong and/or inflation is rising at an uncomfortably high rate, then the Fed can raise interest rates to combat the trend. This move increases the cost of borrowing, encouraging debt pay downs and creating a disincentive to borrow more. This interrelationship supports the normal business cycle: The economy weakens, the Fed lowers rates, credit expands, spending picks up, and the economy improves. Eventually inflation pressures may build and the cycle reverses: The Fed raises rates, credit contracts, spending declines, the economy weakens, and inflation subsides. These cycles have repeated over time, and the sequence is fairly reliable and predictable (of course, the timing is always uncertain).

The Fed's primary instrument of managing short-term interest rates has been an entirely sufficient policy tool during most of modern economic history in the United States. Unfortunately, these are not normal times, because the limits of this policy tool have been reached due to the secular decline in interest rates over the past several decades. Every time there was a material economic slowdown since the 1980s the Fed lowered interest rates, and each subsequent reduction was lower than the previous low. That is, the patient needed more and more medicine until it stopped responding to the standard measure of lowering interest rates. As a result, the doctor now is in need of different medicine to revive the patient.

During the global financial crisis in 2008, the patient was rushed to the emergency room because of a massive heart attack. The doctor first tried to revive the economy with its customary tool of reducing interest rates. The Fed cut rates all the way down to zero for the first time since the Great Depression. The flatlining economy was unresponsive to the maximum dose. That profound statement alone strongly indicates a highly abnormal economic environment. The doctor was forced to reach deeper into its bag and summon stronger, rarely used medicine.

The Fed's Emergency Policy Tool: QE

What can the Fed do to push growth and inflation higher when rates cannot be lowered any further? The playbook eventually used in prior extreme environments like the Great Depression and utilized by other major central banks who faced similar constraints was to attempt to inject new money into the system by purchasing securities using its balance sheet (also known as printing money, quantitative easing, or QE for short). This medicine has material potential side effects and is therefore, only used in emergency situations.

The objective of controlling interest rates is to encourage/discourage borrowing to increase/decrease spending. QE works differently from the Fed's main policy tool. The Fed has the power to inject new money that did not previously exist into the economy. Mechanically, the Fed can't spend the money it prints so the way it introduces new cash into the system is by buying financial assets in the open market. Typically, it buys Treasury bonds with the newly minted money. This exchange puts the bonds on the Fed's balance sheet and the money that was used to purchase the bonds into the hands of the public market seller, which results in new money being introduced into the economic system. One big advantage of buying Treasury bonds with QE is that the Fed can try to control longer-term interest rates (as opposed to the short-term rates they directly manage), since it represents a potentially major source of buying power for longer-dated bonds. More buying can push bond prices up and interest rates down. The benefit of lower rates on long-term bonds is reduced borrowing costs for consumers, businesses, and the government itself. Importantly, interest rates for mortgages and business loans are typically tied directly to longer-term interest rates on government bonds.

As the first sign that the patient was terribly ill, the Fed and many other central banks engaged in QE in early 2009 at the depths of the Global Financial Crisis. This was by necessity, because the normal policy tool of lowering interest rates was insufficient to reverse the economic avalanche precipitated by the housing and financial collapse because interest rates had already been lowered to 0%. Interestingly, the previous time the

Fed started the printing presses was during the Great Depression when rates similarly fell to zero (you may start to notice several disturbing parallels between the current environment and the 1930s as we proceed). The use of QE has ebbed and flowed since 2009, with injections occurring during weakening economic periods and no QE during recoveries. As of this writing, short-term rates are pinned at zero with little expectation of increases any time in the foreseeable future. The Fed has been famously quoted as saying they "are not even thinking about thinking about raising rates," given the pronounced economic stagnation and lack of inflation pressures (of course, these pressures may also turn quickly in the wake of the massive fiscal stimulus in response to COVID-19). Additionally, the extraordinary amount of QE has dwarfed the program established during the Global Financial Crisis, given the magnitude of the economic downturn caused by shutting down the economy amidst the global pandemic.

Similar to lowering interest rates to stimulate the economy, the QE medicine also has limits. It works better when asset prices are low and is less effective when asset prices are higher. Recall that the mechanical process of QE involves the Fed "printing money" and buying financial assets, typically longer-dated government bonds. The sellers of the bonds take the money and buy other assets, which pushes up their prices and helps stimulate the economy as wealth increases. As the yield of the bonds the Fed purchases declines and the prices of the assets others buy increase, the financial enticement to repeat the process diminishes. As the future expected returns of investments fall, there is less incentive to keep buying more assets and more reason to hold on to the cash and not reinvest. Eventually the expected returns of assets are insufficient to compensate investors for the associated risks, and the process stalls.

The Fed's New Policy Tool: Modern Monetary Theory

We are now in uncharted waters. The normal policy tool of controlling interest rates covers most of history, but with rates stuck at zero it is currently impotent. QE has only happened on a few occasions and is quickly reaching its limits. A new third tool, which has never been used at this scale, is often termed Modern Monetary Theory (MMT). Under MMT, the Fed engages in QE and, instead of buying assets in the market, the funds are used to finance government deficits directly. This tool requires coordination between monetary authorities (the Fed) and fiscal policy (Congress). The Fed can "print" the money with approval from its Board of Governors, while Congressional approval involves a complex and challenging political process.

The limits to this innovative medicine are not as clear as those for interest rate cuts and QE, which have more clearly drawn lines, as discussed earlier. Additionally, the potential side effects are less understood given the lack of historical reference. How long can we continue to print money and debase our currency to address our problems without adverse consequence? How productively will the money be spent to help us grow our way out of economic stagnation and pay down our collective debts? Or will we simply end up trying to solve a debt problem with more debt, funding unproductive spending that can't be paid down, which in turn can only be ultimately resolved through inflation or default. The answer to these questions tells us about the limits to this policy tool. Since the mid-1940s the US dollar has enjoyed the honor of serving as the world's reserve currency. This means that the dollar is the main currency the world uses to trade and save. This privilege affords the United States the freedom to print more money than other countries. When I review the history of currencies, I am amazed to learn that just about every major country that held the world's reserve currency eventually relinquished its reserve status after excessive printing. To summarize the past succinctly, countries earn reserve currency status, then abuse that privilege over time by printing more of their currency to resolve their economic troubles, and then eventually give up their reserve status when a more deserving currency emerges. When or if that will happen to the dollar is anyone's guess, but many experts argue that the time of that event may be quickly approaching, even if it takes years to unfold.

Inflation is also a potential limit to MMT as an effective policy tool. When measured inflation is anemic, the cost of printing money is less apparent than when inflation pressures begin to mount. Think of rising inflation as a sign that the patient is showing adverse effects from the medicine. If the patient needs the dosage and isn't demonstrating any issues from taking it, then there's little reason to stop providing the medicine. This is where we stand as of this writing in 2021, recognizing that negative signs may surface at a moment's notice.

There are two central takeaways from the extraordinary measures the Fed has taken to revive the economy. First, the patient clearly exhibits major health problems requiring nontraditional responses. The mere fact that a new tool such as MMT has entered mainstream economic discussions is clear evidence of the uniqueness of the current environment and the gravity of economic conditions. Second, the Fed has unquestionably demonstrated an ability to creatively inject needed stimulus and the willingness to do whatever it takes to keep the patient alive. The Fed is well aware of the major negative pressures the economy faces and has therefore taken extraordinary measures to offset the downward trajectory.

THE DELEVERAGING HEADWIND

The weak economic conditions described earlier in the chapter are symptomatic of a serious pressure most of the developed world faces called deleveraging. The main reason QE ensued during the Great Depression and again since 2009 is this dominant downward stress on growth. We've seen a similar dynamic in Japan from the early 1990s to the present and in Europe since the mid-2000s. Bridgewater refers to this powerful force that is building in the background as the long-term debt cycle. This cycle is less well understood since it only hits its major infection points once or twice in a lifetime. In contrast, the normal business cycle described earlier can turn approximately every three to seven years, making it more observable during typical environments.

When the Fed lowers rates, borrowing increases. When the Fed raises rates, borrowing tends to continue to grow, but at a slower rate, rather than an outright decrease. After all, the economy grows over time, and borrowing constantly fuels our credit-based economy. Think about the last time you or someone you know bought a house or car with cash. These are items that Americans have become accustomed to purchasing on credit. As the normal business cycle proceeds with peaks and troughs and the Fed responds accordingly, a broader long-term debt cycle builds. Contrary to a *self-correcting* normal business cycle, the long-term debt cycle is *self-reinforcing* in nature. This allows debt levels to rise for long stretches of time before reversing and declining for an extended period. The dynamic is self-reinforcing, because the creditworthiness of a borrower is based largely on the value of his or her assets and income. Lenders want to make sure that they can be paid back. The higher the borrower's income and the greater the collateral, the higher the odds of repayment. When we collectively borrow to spend, incomes rise as do the value of our assets. The cycle is virtuous: More borrowing leads to increased spending, which improves incomes and asset values, which are the key factors used by lenders to assess creditworthiness of borrowers, so they lend more. As a result, the total debt burden increases over time, which is different from the self-correcting nature of the regular business cycle (wherein a hot economy is slowed by the Fed's interest rate increases).

The process continues until we hit our debt ceiling, the point at which we simply can't borrow anymore because we can't afford the interest payments. At that juncture, we are no longer creditworthy and have difficulty refinancing our debt and increasing our borrowing. Our aggregate balance sheet is too highly levered relative to our assets and income. Our borrowing relative to our assets and income must be reduced over time. This can happen by reducing the numerator, which is the amount borrowed, or increasing denominator, which is our assets and income, or some combination of both. The process is known as *deleveraging*. Figure 10.1 illustrates the total debt level of the United States (including government, household and business) over the past 100-plus years. It compares total debt to the total income of the country, which is commonly measured using potential nominal gross domestic product (GDP).

Figure 10.1 US Total Debt as a Percentage of Potential Nominal GDP (1915–2020)

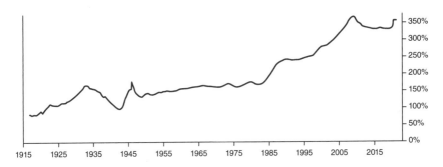

Source: Bridgewater Associates.

Notice the rise in total debt to GDP from the early 1900s to the peak just before the Great Depression in the 1930s. The process shifted into reverse for the next 15 years as the debt to GDP ratio declined until the war, before pivoting again. The last cycle lasted over 60 years as debt rose from the mid-1940s to 2008 when we ostensibly hit our ceiling once again, this time about double the level on a percentage basis previously reached before the Great Depression. One way we know we reached a peak is that cutting interest rates to zero did not trigger the normal response of increased borrowing. There was simply too much debt with insufficient margin of safety already, so lowering rates further did not provoke the expected result, because lenders didn't want to lend to less creditworthy borrowers. This was painfully evident in 2008 as interest rates hit zero for the first time since the 1930s and we were headed into a second devastating depression as the economy screeched to a halt. Not until the Fed turned to the printing presses in March 2009 did the economy cease its decline. Without extraordinary policy efforts to provide liquidity and support to the economy, we could have easily repeated the destructive economic pain experienced in the 1930s.

When the cycle of debt accumulation shifts into reverse, that environment is termed deleveraging. It is an inescapable process that will adjust over time as debt limits are reached. The self-reinforcing nature of the long-term debt cycle prevails in the opposite direction. I can't borrow anymore, so I spend less than I spent before. My reduced spending brings down your income, so you spend less, and that in turn negatively impacts someone else's income. The reduced aggregate spending and selling of assets to pay down debt also drives down asset prices, which hurts the value of borrowers' collateral, further degrading their ability to borrow and spend.

The self-feeding reinforcing dynamic naturally creates significant headwinds to growth and exerts material downward pressure on inflation. Every economy that borrows too much eventually goes through this painful process to readjust its balance sheet, just as an individual or company would. Oftentimes these periods result in depressions, as we saw in the United States in the 1930s and as Japan has suffered over the past 30 years since it hit its debt limit in the early 1990s. Both extended periods were characterized by sluggish growth and low inflation or outright deflation.

The negative pressures presented here may last for a while. The United States' deleveraging process commenced in 2008, and deleveraging has continued at a slow pace since then. The last time we suffered through a similar experience (i.e., the Great Depression), it spanned over a decade until it was ended by a world war. The level of debt we face today is about double where we were before the Great Depression, which suggests that we probably have a long way to go. The pace of deleveraging since 2008 has also been relatively slow and inconsistent and is a sign that we may be in a prolonged process that could pose headwinds for some time to come.

RISE OF POPULISM

Concurrent with a challenging set of economic conditions, rising wealth inequality has unleashed a powerful wave of populism around the world. From the United Kingdom's vote to withdraw from the European Union (Brexit) to the election of populist leaders around the world (such as Donald Trump in the United States), populism is unquestionably on the rise. The widening gap between the haves and the have-nots has fueled the growing sentiment against the establishment, as the voice of the underserved has grown louder. The implementation of QE has only intensified the divide, because the biggest beneficiaries of printing money and buying assets are asset holders and owners of capital (i.e., the rich). The majority of society has not similarly enjoyed the benefits of the economic recovery, because wages have generally been flat since 2009 (as of early 2021).

The rise of populist sentiment increases political uncertainty. In the United States, we are witnessing growing political conflict, with many long-term measures indicating a wider partisan divide than at any point since the Civil War. This makes passing stimulative legislation more challenging, because the environment is more susceptible to political gridlock. When the Fed could unilaterally cut interest rates to stimulate the economy or turn on the printing presses and buy assets on a moment's notice, there was a mechanism in place to respond to economic weakness in a timely manner. Given that the economy is dependent on greater monetary and fiscal coordination than in past years, this potential roadblock introduces greater variability in the economic outcome of future years.

THE NET OUTCOME OF MAJOR HEADWINDS AND TAILWINDS IS HIGHLY UNCERTAIN

In short, there are major forces at play, many of which are unprecedented in size. The massive deflationary forces of an overindebted economy that is in the early stages of its deleveraging cycle pose an immense headwind to growth and inflation. Technological advances have radically improved efficiencies and replaced many jobs with computers. This also has a significant deflationary impact on global economies. Finally, although hopefully shorter-term in nature, the sheer abruptness and magnitude of the economic collapse caused by COVID-19 serves as a highly deflationary force over the near term that is being addressed with massive stimulus to offset the contraction, as discussed below. Although several vaccines are now available, the efficacy and durability of immunity provided and the timeline for true global distribution are still unknown as of this writing.

On the other side, are potentially overwhelming inflationary forces that are equally unprecedented in scale. As the deflationary pressures are well known and felt across the globe, the policy responses to these conditions have been enormous. The Fed and other major central banks have commissioned all the policy tools used in prior recessions (cutting rates to zero and implementing QE) and have creatively augmented their arsenal with new forceful measures (Modern Monetary Theory). Add to that massive fiscal stimulus, ongoing supply chain disruptions, the looming prospect of trade wars, a tightening labor market (with many potential workers being paid more in subsidies not to work), and rising commodity prices as of 2021, and the aggregate inflationary pressure is substantial.

The simple fact that inflation across the standard basket of goods and services used by the majority of Americans has not materially increased to date demonstrates the challenges central banks face in generating inflation (which is a far better outcome than deflation due to the difficulty in escaping a deflationary spiral). Nevertheless, zero or negative interest rates across most of the developed world plus trillions of dollars of printing since 2009 have not stoked inflation (outside of asset prices). The surprising result is that, because the deflationary forces that the policy responses target to combat are so powerful, the net result thus far has been low inflation that has remained low. Recognizing the magnitude of the deleveraging that must be overcome, central bankers have resolved to take whatever measures are necessary to combat it.

How this ultimately ends is very difficult to predict. We could easily experience high inflation from all the QE, as many market pundits fear. Alternatively, the low inflation period in which we currently live may persist should the QE and fiscal stimulus ultimately be insufficient to offset the enormous downward pressures. As mentioned earlier, the messy process of congressional budget approvals introduces added uncertainty, because elected politicians control spending. Even outright deflation is a possibility, similar to what Japan and Europe have suffered despite repeated heroic attempts to escape the entrenched deflationary spiral. Economic growth could easily rebound to normal levels from the attempted stimulus, but we could slip into another recession or even depression if government efforts prove inadequate. The fact that we are more dependent on a coordinated effort between monetary and fiscal authorities raises the odds of a policy accident derailing the economy. Finally, we must consider the probability that the economic environment may constantly shift as the various pressures ebb and flow. Managing these massive forces is no easy task, and the economy is susceptible to unstable conditions as a result.

Not only are the economic results uncertain and likely to change over time, but there is also undeniably an increased risk of *extreme* outcomes. We should not ignore the potential impact of outcomes such as MMT not being enough to resuscitate the patient, leaving no backup plan in place. What if the United States loses its reserve currency status? What would that mean for the global economy? What if there is a loss of faith in paper money – what will emerge as a reliable storehold of wealth? What if new, vaccine-resistant strains of the coronavirus emerge, and we face new challenges in the form of COVID-22, COVID-23, or COVID-24?

Recognizing the uncertainty of the economic environment of tomorrow supports the notion that investors would be wise to maintain a well-balanced portfolio. It is a dangerous strategy to try to predict which environment will transpire and to position for that single outcome. If you happen to guess wrong, you risk a significant loss of capital. Consider that a portfolio that is hedged against rising inflation may be very different from one that is designed to protect against a deflationary depression. In short, the risk parity portfolio presented here is designed to be resilient in varying economic environments, which seems particularly timely given all of the considerations shared in this chapter.

THE NEED FOR LIQUIDITY, LOW FEES, AND TAX EFFICIENCY

Finally, the current environment supports the need for a portfolio that is liquid, has low fees, and is highly tax efficient. Liquidity is important because of the wide range of potential outcomes and the odds of extreme results. A fully liquid portfolio provides investors with the option to pivot as needed or raise cash to fund any needs that may unexpectedly emerge. In contrast, if one gives up liquidity in exchange for hopes of higher returns, then the risk is that an adverse environment transpires and the investor is not able to change course. In other words, there is considerable value in having strong liquidity, and it should only be given up if the upside of doing so is substantial.

In addition, with interest rates pinned at zero and future returns diminished, the impact of fees has increased. All asset-class returns are reduced by lower cash yields. Therefore, the forward-looking long-term returns across the board are likely lower than historical averages. The excess return above cash may be similar to that in the past, but the prospective total return is probably lower. Yet, for the most part, asset management fees have not been meaningfully reduced – certainly not in any way proportionate to the decline in expected returns. The fees you pay for your investments come off the top, and the lower the total return, the greater the percentage those fees represent. In fact, since fees are typically charged on total assets, rather than returns, fees can potentially exceed the return when returns are lower. Thus, there should be a focus on keeping fees as low as possible for a certain level of expected return.

For taxable investors, perhaps the biggest factor now and in the future is tax rates. There is increasing pressure for tax rates to increase over time given the unprecedented levels of fiscal deficits and growing concerns about the rich not paying their fair share. Like fees, taxes reduce the net returns left to the investor and can represent a significant cost. Thus, a renewed focus on tax-efficient portfolios is justified in the current environment.

In sum, you should seek a portfolio that is well balanced, with ample liquidity, low fees, and high tax efficiency. Such a portfolio should provide the desired balanced exposure to public markets and offer attractive returns over time, net of all costs to investors.

CHAPTER ELEVEN

———————◆———————

The Rebalancing Boost

A widely underappreciated benefit of investing in a well-diversified mix of volatile assets is the return boost that can accrue to the total portfolio over time. The extra return is derived from regular rebalancing, which I think of as a repeated process of buying low and selling high. I referred to this bonus earlier in the book. In this chapter, I fully explain the rebalancing boost. My goal is to demonstrate yet another advantage of a risk parity portfolio that goes beyond diversification as a risk-reducing strategy but also as a way to enhance returns.

CONCEPTUAL FRAMEWORK: BUY LOW, SELL HIGH

Everyone loves to receive a big discount when purchasing goods and services. We have all seen the rush that ensues when a huge sale has been announced. Paying less than fair value is universally preferred over paying a higher price. It should be no different with investments where the first lesson taught is to buy low and sell high.

In practice, however, this can be challenging to execute, because our emotions tend to tug us in the opposite direction. When something is performing poorly, our defensive impulse is to sell to curtail the pain associated with losses. Likewise, while an asset is appreciating, the fear of missing out compels us to buy even though the price has already risen. Therefore, most investors are more likely to buy high and sell low than to follow the golden rule laid out earlier. Thus, the goal of this section is to demonstrate the mathematical benefits of regular rebalancing to enable you to overcome the emotional pull that can lead to poor results.

From a conceptual standpoint, think about the return boost that comes from rebalancing in the following way. Imagine that we have two assets that earn identical average returns over the full period. Importantly, these two assets go up and down at different times. Therefore, periods of outperformance are inevitably followed by stretches of underperformance relative to their respective averages and vice versa for each asset. In reality, markets tend to exaggerate up and down periods and then correct back to the long-term trend. Importantly, diverse asset classes will follow different paths during this process, creating the opportunity to benefit from rebalancing. By trimming after strong relative returns and adding after relatively poor results, you proactively adjust the base along the way. The base shrinks after good returns and increases following underperformance. In other words, rebalancing results in a repeated process of buying when prices are low and selling after they have risen. More capital is at risk before above-average returns and less is invested before below-average results. That process logically leads to more dollars in the end than if no changes were made along the way.

The following example consisting of a simple two-asset portfolio will illustrate the extra return achieved with even a single rebalance. You invest $100 in asset 1 and after two years it is worth $120. Your investment in asset 2 also increases from $100 to $120 over the same two-year period, but through a different return path. Asset 1 may have a good year when asset 2 underperforms and vice versa. If you invest $100 in each of these two assets and do not reallocate for two years, you'd end up with $240 total (since each is worth $120 at the end).

Instead, let's say that you rebalance the portfolio back to its starting 50/50 allocation after the first year as opposed to leaving each asset alone. If asset 1 appreciates 20% in year 1, and asset 2 earns 0%, then you would have $120 in asset 1 and $100 in asset 2 for a total portfolio worth $220. To get back to an equal mix in each asset, you would have to sell $10 of asset 1 and buy $10 of asset 2 (to get each to $110, which is half of $220). This rebalancing process is summarized in Table 11.1.

Table 11.1   Rebalancing After Year 1

Asset	Starting Value	Earnings Year 1	Rebalancing at End of Year	Ending Value
1	$100	20% (or $20)	Sell $10	$110
2	$100	0% (or $0)	Buy $10	$110
Total Portfolio	$200	10% (or $20)	–	$220

Note: Hypothetical scenario provided for illustrative purposes only.

In year 2 the opposite returns transpire: asset 1 is flat and asset 2 gains 20%. Table 11.2 illustrates the results after the second year.

Table 11.2   Ending Value After Year 2

Asset	Starting Value	Earnings Year 2	Ending Value
1	$110	0% (or $0)	$110
2	$110	20% (or $22)	$132
Total Portfolio	**$220**	**10% (or $22)**	**$242**

Note: Hypothetical scenario provided for illustrative purposes only.

By rebalancing after year 1 you were able to achieve an ending portfolio value of $242. This is $2 more than the $240 that would have been the result of statically holding both assets for two years. The extra $2, which amounts to 0.8%, is the extra return that came from rebalancing across the exact same assets over two years. Over time, the rebalancing boost can compound to yield significant benefits without incurring excess risk. It's another "free lunch" that investors can capture with a plain rebalancing program.

LOW CORRELATION AND HIGH VOLATILITY

The rebalancing boost is greater the lower the correlation between assets and the higher the volatility of each asset. The low correlation benefit should be clear. If two assets move in tandem, then they will both tend to outperform and underperform their averages around the same time. This would leave little opportunity to buy low and sell high since both would likely be low or high concurrently.

The advantage of higher volatility is likely underappreciated. To demonstrate the improvement in the rebalancing boost that comes from owning more volatile assets, we will use the same two asset portfolio as earlier. This time we will increase the volatility of each asset while holding the total return the same.

In this new example, asset 1 gains 25% in the first year while asset 2 loses 4% (versus the +20% and 0% returns in our previous example). In year 2, the two assets experience the opposite returns (asset 1 loses 4% and asset 2 gains 25%). If no changes are made between years 1 and 2, then the total portfolio would be worth the exact same $240 as in our first example. To see the improvement from the rebalancing boost, we will now follow the same process as before by rebalancing these two assets at the end of year 1. Table 11.3 provides a summary.

Table 11.3   Rebalancing After Year 1 – More Volatile Assets

Asset	Starting Value	Earnings Year 1	Rebalancing at End of Year	Ending Value
1	$100	25% (or $25)	Sell $14.50	$110.50
2	$100	–4% (or –$4)	Buy $14.50	$110.50
Total Portfolio	$200	10.5% (or $21)	–	$221

Note: Hypothetical scenario provided for illustrative purposes only.

You can see the return boost after year 2 in Table 11.4.

Table 11.4   Ending Value After Year 2 – More Volatile Assets

Asset	Starting Value	Earnings Year 2	Ending Value
1	$110.50	–4% (or –$4.42)	$106.08
2	$110.50	25% (or $27.63)	$138.13
Total Portfolio	$221	10.5% (or $23.21)	$244.21

Note: Hypothetical scenario provided for illustrative purposes only.

In the more-volatile example with rebalancing, we end with $244.21, which is 1.8% more than our nonrebalanced portfolio's ending value of $240. The 1.8% is also 1% greater than the rebalancing boost from our first example. The reason the improvement was so great was because we increased the base of an asset just before a huge gain and reduced the allocation to an asset immediately preceding a big loss. If the gain/loss were smaller, the benefit from rebalancing would have been materially reduced (as can be seen by comparing the boost to our first example).

This is a very important point that bears repeating, because it can be counterintuitive and fly in the face of many investment tenets that have been taught. We have two portfolios that would yield the exact same dollar return without rebalancing. The second consists of assets that are more volatile than the first (and similarly correlated). Given these facts, the vast majority of investors would opt for the less volatile assets that provide the same expected return. However, as our simple rebalancing exercise demonstrates, the more-volatile asset mix actually produces more dollars!

THE REBALANCING BOOST APPLIED TO THE RISK PARITY PORTFOLIO

The risk parity portfolio is well positioned to take full advantage of the rebalancing boost. It is invested in a diverse set of asset classes that are biased to outperform during various economic environments. That is, the assets are fundamentally designed to exhibit low correlation to one another. Moreover, we attempt to increase the volatility of each asset to match equities, which means everything we own is highly volatile.

We can roughly calculate the rebalancing boost in the risk parity portfolio by comparing the weighted average returns of the underlying asset classes to the actual returns of a portfolio of the same assets that are regularly rebalanced. Table 11.5 lists the historical total returns of the asset classes in our risk parity portfolio since 1998.

Table 11.5   Risk Parity Portfolio Asset-Class Returns – April 1998 to March 2021

Asset Class	Allocation Percentage	Average Returns
US Equities	12.5%	8.0%
Non-US Developed Equities	5.0%	4.6%
Emerging Market Equities	7.5%	7.4%
Long-Term Treasuries	35.0%	6.5%
Long-Term TIPS	35.0%	7.2%
Commodities		
60% Commodity Producers	*15.0%*	*9.1%*
40% Gold	*10.0%*	*7.8%*
Risk Parity Portfolio*	**120.0%**	**9.2%**
Weighted Average Return*		**8.3%**

*Risk parity portfolio return and weighted average return each include negative 20% exposure to cash to account for and Evoke Advisors analysis the cost of leverage using Treasury futures.
Source: Bloomberg and Evoke Advisors analysis.

Notice that the risk parity portfolio earned 9.2% per annum since 1998 while the weighted average return of the underlying asset classes came in at 8.3%. The only difference between these two measures is the risk parity portfolio rebalanced once per month. This repeated process yielded an improvement just shy of 1% per year for 23 years. As mentioned before, even more impressive is the fact that the 9.2% is greater than any single asset-class return, which is a clear demonstration of the benefits of rebalancing (and of using some cheap leverage).

One other point is worth mentioning. Recall that the risk parity portfolio invests in long-duration Treasuries and TIPS and applies some leverage to those positions to further increase their expected risk and return. As mentioned, this is done to better balance the portfolio by enabling all assets to have comparable upside to offset underperformance in the other areas. It also improves the expected return of the total portfolio since every component is structured to deliver equity-like returns over time. That step increases the expected return of the total portfolio to be competitive with equities over the long run.

In this chapter I have introduced another benefit that bumps the expected return up another 0.5% to 1.0% per year. Since the risk parity portfolio is invested in a diversified mix of lowly correlated and highly volatile assets, it is well positioned for an attractive rebalancing boost on top of the equity-like expected return from its underlying holdings. By increasing the volatility of Treasuries and TIPS, we not only get them to a higher expected return as a stand-alone investment, but we also improve the rebalancing boost to the total portfolio.

SUMMARY

The risk parity portfolio actually has an expected return that is slightly better than equities even though each of its holdings is structured to have a return competitive with equities. The rebalancing boost can add up to 1% per year over an extended period of time from a regular process of buying low and selling high among individually volatile, lowly correlated assets.

All this, of course, assumes that rebalancing is actually implemented. In my 20+ years of experience advising clients, the most difficult part about taking advantage of the rebalancing boost is overcoming the emotional response to sell when you should be buying and vice versa. I have found that an effective approach to implement this strategy in practice is to set an automatic periodic rebalancing process. For instance, once every year (or quarter or any frequency desired) on a specific date, rebalance the risk parity portfolio back to its target allocation. By definition, this means that you would trim a little from the outperformers since the last rebalancing (sell high) and add to the underperformers (buy low). The automatic, rules-based process helps remove the timing aspect of the rebalancing, which could easily be influenced by emotional impulses about future market direction. An even better solution would be taking the decision entirely out of the investors' hands by implementing rebalancing within a managed vehicle. This way the emotional blockage can potentially be completely eliminated. The next chapter on implementation will cover some of these topics in greater detail.

CHAPTER TWELVE

Efficient Implementation

Conventional investment wisdom posits that there is a logical trade-off between risk and return. If you want to seek greater returns you must take more risk in one form or another. As such, the risk parity framework, which has a long-term expected return competitive with equities but with much less risk, is often met with skepticism and disbelief. At the same time, the idea that a portfolio only made up of assets with equity-like returns should perform in line with equities (if not better) over the long run is perfectly reasonable. With this portfolio, investors would not need to sacrifice returns for risk reduction in the same way as they would with the traditional approach. The long-term historical data certainly proves this out.

Instead, the scaling up and down of risk comes in the form of how much or little to allocate to the total risk parity portfolio versus cash as opposed to shifting between lower- and higher-risk assets within the portfolio. Investors who wish to take less risk than that of the risk parity portfolio can allocate more assets to cash and leave less in risk parity. This would in effect lower the total portfolio risk to the desired level. Similarly, those who seek even greater returns can take the added step of leveraging the risk parity portfolio to earn excess returns above the cost of borrowing on top of the high expected returns of the strategy.

The risk parity approach is generally not well understood or widely followed even though many of the most sophisticated investors in the world have fully adopted the concepts. This fact makes actually implementing the risk parity portfolio in practice more difficult than if it was more conventional. The main reason is psychological in nature, as the reference point for comparison of its short-term performance is normally equities or the traditional 60/40 mix. The issue is that the risk parity portfolio's returns will often diverge from commonly used benchmarks since the latter are invested in different assets.

Not only do investors need to grapple with the emotions associated with periods of underperformance relative to equities or 60/40, but they also need to be able to stare at individual line items in the portfolio that may be doing poorly. Emotionally they may feel the need to sell the losers, while a more successful long-term strategy requires buying at the lows. This goes back to the rebalancing boost mentioned in the previous chapter. We establish a balanced allocation with the plan to regularly rebalance back to the target. This process requires selling a portion of the outperformers, because their good returns increased the allocation to those assets, and buying the underperformers for the opposite reason. This can be exceptionally challenging to execute in practice because, normally, concerning news and pessimistic outlooks accompany poor returns.

For these reasons, the implementation plan for adopters of the risk parity framework warrants discussion. The assets used in our risk parity portfolio are limited to easily accessible, liquid, large public markets. These qualities allow for extremely efficient implementation of the strategy. Moreover, investors must recognize that a potential challenge in adopting this asset allocation approach is the requirement of holding individual line items that may be difficult to emotionally justify when they are inevitably performing poorly. Finally, low cost, tax efficiency (for taxable investors) and the ability to leverage (for those interested) are also important considerations.

Factoring in all these objectives, one of the most efficient vehicles to utilize for implementing risk parity is an exchange traded fund (ETF). ETFs were first developed in the 1990s as a way to provide a broad range of investors access to passive index funds.[1] Since then, ETFs have become one of the most popular investment vehicles both for individual as well as institutional investors. Risk parity within an ETF structure offers several advantages relative to building the same strategy on a separate account basis or through a mutual fund vehicle. Next, I walk through the key considerations in implementing a risk parity strategy, including the reasons I favor an ETF structure.

---

[1] https://www.investopedia.com/articles/exchangetradedfunds/12/brief-history-exchange-traded-funds.asp

SIMPLICITY

Even for those who fully adopt the approach and understand the concepts, implementing risk parity can be an involved process. Investors have to decide which individual securities or funds to buy and how often to rebalance. Some investments may have high minimums or not be available on the platform on which the investor holds their assets. Additionally, the investor would need to know how to cost-effectively buy and sell shares and which share classes of each fund to target.

For all these reasons, there may be strong interest in buying a single risk parity fund as opposed to individually trying to figure out which underlying assets to choose. A risk parity fund offers immediate access to, and professional management of, the risk parity strategy with a single purchase. In terms of simplicity, either a mutual fund or ETF would suffice, because both are commingled vehicles that take over the decision-making process.

HIDDEN LINE ITEMS

Perhaps the biggest benefit of implementation of risk parity within a commingled vehicle, be it an ETF or a mutual fund, is the artificial masking of the performance of the individual holdings. This is because the package of the holdings is far easier to hold on to than the individual line items. Daniel Kahneman, in his famous book *Thinking, Fast and Slow*, offers a brilliant explanation for the way people tend to view decision-making. He explains the difference between "broad framing" and "narrow framing," where the former refers to taking each decision within the context of the bigger picture, whereas the latter involves seeing each decision in isolation. By focusing on the overall portfolio rather than on the individual line items, investors are less likely to react to their detriment.

Consider that our total risk parity portfolio consists of asset classes, each of which has comparable return and risk as equities. This means that the holdings are volatile! We've all lived through the challenges of holding equities during a severe downturn. The difficulty of not selling at the lows is many times greater for other asset classes. This is because most investors are used to the volatility of equities. The losing periods are well covered by popular media, and there are countless supporters of the strategy of buying stocks on dips to help walk investors off the ledge when emotions are running high. The other asset classes typically do not have similar backing, largely because the majority of investors don't structure them to have higher returns and risk. However, the package of the asset classes can be very attractive, because the combination exhibits much lower volatility than the underlying components. Therefore, hiding the line items within a fund makes it more likely that investors will exercise broad framing, hold on to the strategy, and benefit over the long run from rebalancing into underperforming asset classes.

LOW COST

ETFs are widely considered the low-cost option for investors. According to Morningstar, the average ETF annual expense ratio in 2016 was 0.23%, compared to the average expense ratio of 0.73% for index mutual funds.[2] This is by far the most important measure of cost for long-term investors as the annual difference in expenses compounds over time. Mutual funds may also charge a "load" of 1–2% on top of the annual expenses. ETFs do not have loads as they are directly traded on the stock exchange similar to a stock. There may be small commissions charged for purchasing and selling ETFs on the exchange, but many custodians like Charles Schwab, Fidelity, and Vanguard have recently waived commissions for ETF buys and sells. The trend is clearly moving toward zero commissions industry wide. One difference between mutual funds and ETFs is that mutual funds trade at net asset value (NAV), whereas ETFs trade at the market price, which can fluctuate below or above NAV. For ETFs that invest in liquid, public markets, the spread between the market price and NAV is generally very narrow since market makers have the ability to arbitrage the difference for a risk-free return. This opportunity typically tightens the spread.

HIGH LIQUIDITY

ETFs can be traded intraday, whereas mutual funds can only be bought and sold at the day's closing price. Additionally, the ongoing ability of market makers to arbitrage generally makes ETFs highly liquid, since they effectively tap into the liquidity of the underlying markets in which they hold securities. This even applies to thinly traded ETFs. In fact, large ETF orders can potentially be handled directly with an authorized participant who can create or redeem shares of the ETF outside of the normal daily trading volume for shares of the ETF itself. These channels help make it relatively easy to transact in an ETF, regardless of the daily trading volume, as long as the securities the ETF holds are themselves relatively liquid.

---

[2] https://www.fidelity.com/learning-center/investment-products/etf/etfs-cost-comparison

LOW TAXES

One of the biggest advantages of an ETF structure versus either a mutual fund or a separately managed account employing the exact same risk parity strategy is lower taxes. ETFs can be vastly more tax efficient than a separate account or competing mutual funds.[3] An individual security within the risk parity portfolio that is sold for a profit creates a capital gain. These sales can result either from an effort to rebalance or to meet redemptions/distributions. Capital gains would normally generate taxes even though the investor in the risk parity strategy may not have reduced their position in the fund or sold any shares of the risk parity mutual fund or ETF. Whether the investor actually incurs these taxes can depend on the structure of the investment.

Separately managed account investors are responsible for paying taxes for all the net gains created from the changes within their portfolio every year. Similarly, mutual funds are required to distribute capital gains to underlying investors at the end of the year even if the holder of the mutual fund never sold a share. ETFs, on the other hand, are structurally different from mutual funds. Mutual funds must sell securities to raise cash to meet client redemptions. This forces a sale of securities, which may generate a capital gain. However, when an individual investor in an ETF wants to sell, he or she simply sells shares to another investor as they would with a stock and does not generate capital gains within the ETF. For larger redemptions, the ETF issuer has the option to redeem in kind by distributing holdings within the ETF without having to sell and generate a capital gain.[4] The same can be done for rebalancing to minimize taxes within an ETF structure.

Given the ETF's tax advantages, investors will typically not have to realize significant capital gains until they themselves decide to sell their appreciated shares.

TRANSPARENCY

Some investors may be interested in having the ability to look at the individual holdings of the risk parity strategy at any time. Full transparency can provide comfort to those who are used to seeing every holding in their portfolio.

ETFs typically disclose all individual holdings on a daily basis on their public website. This allows investors to know exactly what they are

[3] https://www.etf.com/etf-education-center/etf-basics/why-are-etfs-so-tax-efficient
[4] https://www.etf.com/etf-education-center/etf-basics/why-are-etfs-so-tax-efficient

holding at any point in time. Therefore, investors can receive the afore-mentioned benefits of holding risk parity within a commingled vehicle while maintaining the same transparency as a separate account.

Contrast this to a mutual fund that normally reports underlying positions on a quarterly basis. Mutual-fund disclosures are also often lagged 30 days or longer, which potentially leaves investors in the dark for a longer period of time.

LEVERAGE

One of the ways risk parity is able to allocate across a diverse mix of assets while maintaining an equity-plus expected return is through the modest use of leverage. This component of the strategy introduces two additional important implementation considerations: (1) the cost of leverage and (2) potential administrative hurdles to employing leverage in practice.

These two complications provide an additional advantage of using commingled funds (ETFs and mutual funds) as preferred implementation vehicles. Within a fund structure, the manager can take the administrative burdens off the investor with implementation efficiencies that come from professional management. For instance, an investor who seeks to use leverage may be limited to borrowing on margin. This approach potentially exposes the investor to higher borrowing costs and possible margin calls that would require adding cash or selling securities to cover during downturns. Within a fund, the manager can make these decisions to maximize the return and minimize the risk and taxes generated within the strategy.

The cost and accessibility of leverage is also a significant differentiator. Most brokerage accounts are limited to using margin to access leverage. Within a fund, the manager can use derivatives in the form of futures or swaps to effectively and efficiently employ leverage. This method typically has lower financing costs, which results in a higher net return to the investor.

SUMMARY

This chapter concludes the insights about constructing a risk parity portfolio that I wanted to share with you. I have described the conceptual framework at length to help build confidence in the long-term viability of the overall approach. I walked you through the steps to constructing a well-balanced portfolio of diverse asset classes. The historical data over multiple decades was presented to demonstrate that the strategy has worked well for a very long period of time and through various economic environments.

In the final two chapters I plan to discuss when the risk parity portfolio may not perform well. With any investment strategy, it is critical to be fully knowledgeable about the downside as well as the upside. Having this insight upfront makes it less likely that you will experience a negative surprise that may potentially cause you to sell at an inopportune time. I will also dive into a wide range of common questions that I have received over the years.

CHAPTER THIRTEEN

When Does Risk Parity Underperform?

Periods of underperformance are inevitable for any strategy, including risk parity. From an absolute return standpoint, no mix of risky asset classes with a high expected return can successfully avoid interim periods of losses over the long run. A more realistic goal is to minimize the downturns as opposed to attempting to completely eliminate them.

From a *relative* perspective, underperformance can occur more frequently if the reference point is the stock market, which can enjoy remarkable upswings from time to time. A more balanced asset allocation, even one that is designed to beat stocks over the long run, will certainly trail a 100% stock holding when equities are the best-performing asset class.

I have been implementing the risk parity approach with my clients for over a decade. Over that time, I have witnessed firsthand investor reactions to stretches of underperformance. This experience is crucial, because investors are human and are therefore susceptible to acting on their emotions. For these reasons, I devote this entire chapter to explaining the types of environments when you should expect the risk parity portfolio to perform poorly. I will mostly address underperformance through an absolute-return lens, because that is most relevant, but I will also touch on relative returns because I recognize the temptation to view returns that way.

BREAK GLASS IN CASE OF EMERGENCY

Assuming you have bought into the risk parity framework and are planning to invest using this philosophy, there will inevitably come a time when you may be tempted to change your mind. Such an event will most likely occur when the strategy is performing poorly (as very few investors opt to get out of a strategy that is doing well). When you feel the urge to abandon the approach, you should reread this chapter. You can think of it as a resource in the event of an emergency (also known as a period of poor returns).

This book was obviously printed before the underperformance that you lived through transpired. If the text clearly articulates the environment in which the underperformance occurred and why underperformance should be expected, then that should hopefully help you hold on through the downturn. In other words, if we acknowledge that every strategy will suffer through bad periods and we can understand what those environments look like, then we should be less prone to selling (and ultimately buying) at those lows. This serves as the goal of this chapter.

RISKY ASSETS VERSUS CASH

Investors have a basic choice when deciding to invest. They can take the risk-free rate (largely set by the Fed) and not risk capital loss. If cash is yielding 4%, they can just leave their money in cash and earn the 4%. But if the goal is to earn more than cash, then investors can take risk with their capital by allocating to a number of different risky asset classes. By thoughtfully diversifying across these asset classes, as shown in prior chapters, the risk of material loss and volatility can be minimized. This certainly does not mean that risk is completely eliminated. Indeed, there are numerous instances of negative calendar-year *excess* returns above cash over the past 50 years as summarized in Table 13.1.

Table 13.1   Negative Calendar-Year Excess Returns for Risk Parity – Since January 1970

Year	Return	Year	Return	Year	Return
1975	−0.3%	1990	−11.4%	2001	−2.6%
1977	−1.2%	1992	−1.0%	2008	−14.6%
1981	−28.3%	1994	−7.2%	2013	−10.3%
1983	−6.4%	1996	−2.2%	2015	−8.8%
1984	−10.2%	1997	−1.9%	2018	−8.9%

Source: Bloomberg.

On only five occasions in over 50 years did the risk parity portfolio underperform cash by 10% or more (1981, 1984, 1990, 2008, 2013), and only once did it trail cash by over 15% (1981) in a calendar year. (On a total return basis, the observed downside would have been much less painful. For instance, cash earned over 16% in 1981, which would have emotionally alleviated a big portion of the –28% excess return that year.)

Regardless, the question is this: In what environments is a risk parity portfolio expected to underperform cash? This is the most relevant reference point because if it does worse than cash, then you could have just held cash and not taken any risk. This represents a higher bar than comparing returns versus zero, because cash is nearly always above zero.

CASH IS KING DURING TWO ENVIRONMENTS

There are two general types of environments when cash tends to outperform all risky assets: when cash rates unexpectedly rise and during periods of panic. As such, these would represent unfavorable environments for the risk parity portfolio, which merely consists of a diversified mix of risky asset classes. Note that we are referring to periods longer than a single day or even a week. Obviously, volatile securities can fluctuate without full explanation as buyers and sellers trade shares over shorter time frames. However, over longer periods, returns are, by and large, reflective of the economic environments. To this point, I have discussed the influence of growth and inflation on asset-class returns. Here I will address the attractiveness of cash as an additional factor that can influence asset-class prices. It is important for you to be aware of this factor even though it is rarely material and doesn't last long when it is relevant.

1. Cash Rates Unexpectedly Rise

Previously I had explained that risky asset classes offer a risk premium above cash. If that were not the case, then no one would rationally invest in that asset class. Why take risk if the expected return is the same or lower than risk-free cash? Thus, all assets effectively compete with cash. The less attractive the yield of cash, the lower the required expected return of asset classes to entice investment. Likewise, as cash rates rise and become more attractive, so should the expected return of risky assets rise (as prices fall) to adequately compensate investors for taking risk.

Imagine if the interest rate offered by cash is 1%. Equities have delivered about 5% above cash over the past 100 years. If we assume an average excess return looking forward, a reasonable expectation for equities with cash yielding 1% would be about 6%. Now consider if the Fed announced tomorrow that it had raised the yield of cash from 1% to 10%. If you were an investor in stocks, how would you react? You now have a choice of taking significant risk with stocks that have an expected return of 6% or selling the stocks and holding cash that suddenly offers 10% risk free. Clearly, the attractiveness of cash has materially and unexpectedly improved in our example. You would certainly switch from stocks to cash as would other investors. This natural reaction would immediately result in collapsing stock prices that need to reprice relative to the updated cash yield. Maintaining the same risk premium, equities should fall in price to a point that results in a forward-looking expected return of say 15% (5% above the new cash rate, assuming the new rate were expected to persist). The lower the purchase price, the higher the expected return, all else equal. This is because the return is based on what you pay when you buy, and the appreciation and income earned until you sell. When the price falls to this point, then investors will likely be swayed into buying and the market price will clear. None of this is a precise science, because there are multiple moving parts simultaneously impacting prices. The point of this exercise is to take each of these variables in isolation to explain the mechanics of market pricing.

The preceding example involved an unexpected change in the current cash yield. There is another way that cash can influence asset-class prices without actually changing. At any point in time, the price of each asset class is reflective of the current rate of cash *and* the future rate of cash that is expected over time. For instance, the current interest rate offered by a cash investment may be 1% today. We can observe what the market is discounting that cash rate to be in a year from now by looking at the Treasury yield curve. If it is upward sloping (after adjusting for any premium for the longer term of the bond), then that indicates the bond market is pricing the rate of cash to rise over time. This is because an investor should be largely indifferent to holding cash at today's rate and living through the changes in rates that will play out through time and buying a longer-dated Treasury note with a fixed higher rate. For example, if a one-year note was yielding 2% (with cash at 1%), then an investor could just buy the one-year note and hold it until it matures. This will ensure the holder a government-guaranteed return of 2%. Therefore, this market pricing suggests that the expectation is that cash will average a little less than 2% for the full year to make the two investments more or less equivalent. In other words, the expectation is that cash rates will increase from the current 1% rate to above 2% in one year to *average* about 2% for the full term. That is, the market is discounting rising interest rates.

Because neither the one-year note nor cash has risk of default, the only difference between the two investments is the term, meaning that the longer-term bond has some interest rate risk, because rates may rise more than expected, which would result in the cash investor outperforming the note holder. Of course, rates may not rise, in which case the note investor does better. Over time, these differences, by and large, even out. Therefore, the yield curve essentially shows the current expected future shifts in cash rates (minus a modest premium paid to the noteholder for taking interest-rate risk).

Let's say that the Fed doesn't change the current rate of cash but signals that it will raise cash rates in the near future. Or perhaps it doesn't say anything, but the market suddenly anticipates that future cash rates will increase more than what is already discounted. Investors are constantly trying to guess what the Fed will do based on a variety of inputs in an attempt to move ahead of the market for profit. This would also be considered an environment during which cash has become more attractive. Even though current rates have not moved, the expectation of future rates has shifted upward.

In all of these cases, cash has, or is expected to become, more attractive than it was previously. This shift is simultaneously a negative for all asset classes. Since each has to offer an expected return above cash, when cash rates rise more than discounted, this poses a negative and concurrent headwind for all asset-class prices.

A good example of the first type of cash rate increase occurred in 1994. In that year, the Fed surprisingly increased the Fed funds rate by 2.5% after leaving it flat for several years. The years 2013 and 2018 were instances when longer-term interest rates rose as the market started to anticipate that the Fed was going to raise cash rates sooner than originally expected.

All these periods posed a headwind for all risky asset classes. Note that the opposite is also true. When cash rates unexpectedly decline, then a tailwind develops for all asset classes. The logic is the reverse of that just described. Cash becomes less attractive either with actual cash rates falling more than discounted or the market shifting its expectation of future cash rates lower. Less-attractive cash pushes up the value of all risky assets as money flows in because of the relative value that was just created.

There is another way to think about the impact of changes in cash rates on risky assets. An asset's current value generally reflects the value of its future expected cash flows discounted back to the present. To the extent those cash flows are discounted back at a higher rate when cash rates rise, their value falls, and the asset needs to re-price accordingly. The opposite also holds true: the value of assets rises when cash rates decline. That is, a higher risk-free rate requires a higher expected return. When the risk-free rate rises, the discount rate for future expected cash flows also rises, which causes the re-pricing that brings the expected excess return back in line. In addition to this mechanical effect, there may also be knock-on fundamental effects of the higher risk-free rate (e.g., higher borrowing costs may also negatively impact consumer spending and company growth prospects and increase default risk).

2. Panic

The second type of market environment when cash reigns supreme occurs during periods dominated by panic or forced selling. September/October 2008 and March 2020 provide two relatively recent examples. Those were times when investors were terrified of losses and indiscriminately sold assets in favor of holding safe cash. In more extreme cases of panic, there can also be forced selling when investors and banks have no choice but to sell given high leverage levels and the declining value of their collateral and assets. These environments typically occur when there are legitimate events to fear like the global financial crisis or a global pandemic. Another example was 1929 at the beginning of the Great Depression.

These environments do not have to be as extreme as the examples provided. Today the term often used is "risk-off," to indicate shifting investor sentiment toward the safety of cash. Mechanically, what occurs during these times is the premium demanded by investors for taking risk increases. That is, due to fear or uncertainty, investors require greater compensation in the form of higher expected returns to part with the guaranteed return that cash offers. When all assets drop together, then the expected return (or the risk premium above cash) becomes more attractive until it reaches a point when investors jump back in. Note that the term *risk-off* is probably overused and often refers to short bursts when both stocks and bonds simultaneously lose money. There is less emphasis on other diversifying assets such as inflation hedges since these markets are heavily underowned and not as closely followed by the mainstream media.

When cash is king, it makes sense that the risk parity portfolio will underperform. A balanced mix of risky assets that should outperform cash over the long run would naturally fall over a shorter period when the return on cash beats all risky assets. Of course, the opposite risk-on environments that are dominated by fear of missing out and euphoria can provide a positive influence on all assets at the same time. These periods often occur after the downturn when fear is at a peak. The year 2009 and the final three quarters of 2020 offer recent instances of this environment.

RARE AND SHORT-LIVED PERIODS

In terms of frequency, it is important to understand that the two environments just described, during which cash can outperform risky assets (when cash rates unexpectedly rise and during periods of panic), have been rare and short-lived. This is because risky assets should outperform cash over the long run; otherwise capitalism would effectively stall. If an extended period ensued during which all assets underperformed cash, then investors would not invest, and the economic machine would essentially freeze.

Furthermore, some sort of a policy response often follows these environments. The Fed typically steps in to prop up the markets and economy because it understands the longer-term impact of the stoppage of the economic flywheel. The Fed stimulates the economy by lowering interest rates to encourage borrowing to spend or invest. It can also print money either to buy assets or provide funding to the government, which can spend the newly minted currency. These responses generally result in markets gaining their footing and restarting the normal cause-effect linkages. This doesn't mean that stocks stop falling, but it does indicate that growth and inflation conditions once again become more dominant than rising risk premiums. We saw this in late 2008. The markets and economy continued to collapse until the Fed cut rates to zero and announced plans to inject massive stimulus into the system in the form of quantitative easing. Upon this move, the panic ceased, and markets began to function normally once again with the understanding that the "plumbing" of the financial system would be supported and remain intact. Stocks continued the downward trajectory for a while as growth continued to decline, but Treasuries, TIPS, and gold began to rebound. A similar turnaround occurred in March 2020 at the onset of COVID-19 once the Fed and fiscal authorities took action in response to the breakdown in economic activity. To be clear, each panic was triggered by fundamental causes. But these episodes went beyond concerns of weaker growth; they reflected systemic fears about the integrity and ongoing viability of the financial markets and the economy. As a result, all risky assets that depend on that system sold off. This is in contrast to the technology bubble sell-off that began in March 2000, for example, which did not appear to have systemic implications.

CONCEPTUALLY NETTING THE IMPACT TO ASSET-CLASS PRICES

In this chapter I introduced two new factors that may influence asset-class prices: the attractiveness of cash and periods of panic/euphoria. Previously I had explained how shifts in growth and inflation are the major drivers of asset-class returns. We can now *conceptually* net all these factors against one another to come up with the total attribution of asset-class returns. Again, since periods of sharp cash rate increases and panic/euphoria are rare and short-lived, the majority of the time asset-class returns are dominated by growth and inflation changes. However, we should consider all these influences all the time even though, most of the time, the former two have minimal effects.

Each of these forces can transpire at differing levels of magnitude. For example, in the first quarter of 2020 (at the onset of the COVID-19 pandemic), growth dramatically collapsed relative to what had been discounted. This presented a massively negative influence on rising growth assets such as stocks and industrial commodities. Likewise, it proved to be strongly bullish for falling-growth assets like Treasuries, TIPS, and gold. Inflation also fell, but the drop was largely driven by the decline in growth. Thus, falling-inflation assets benefited while rising-inflation hedges took a relative hit to their prices. At the same time, fear and panic dominated investor mindsets, and that negatively impacted all asset-class prices. Table 13.2 summarizes these outcomes alongside returns by marking a single plus or minus for each asset class for minor deviations versus expectations, and a double plus or minus for moves of greater magnitude. A plus indicates a positive environment for that particular asset class and a minus a negative.

Table 13.2   Factors That Impacted Asset-Class Returns – First Quarter 2020

Asset Class	Environment			
	Falling Growth	Falling Inflation/Deflation	Panic	Net Return
Equities	– –	+	–	–21.1%
Long-Term Treasuries	++	++	–	20.9%
Long-Term TIPS	++	–	–	9.4%
Commodities	– –	–	–	–30.9%
Gold	++	–	–	3.9%
Risk Parity Portfolio	**n/a**	**n/a**	**–**	**–0.8%**

Source: Bloomberg.

The returns on the far-right column effectively are a by-product of all the individually referenced influences on the price of the particular asset class. For instance, equities are a rising-growth and falling-inflation-biased asset. During the first quarter of 2020, growth dramatically underperformed expectations, which materially negatively impacts equities (as indicated by the double minus signs in the falling-growth column). Inflation fell (which is normally positive for equities), but there was a period of outright deflation (which is significantly negative for stocks). Finally, there was widespread panic and indiscriminate selling which is why I include a negative for each asset class under Panic. Going from left to right in the equities row, you can see three negatives and just one positive, which conceptually netted out to a significantly negative return for the full period (−21.1%).

Long-term Treasuries, on the other hand, returned nearly the exact opposite result during the quarter (+20.9%). Treasuries were similarly impacted by the panic that ensued. It got two pluses for falling inflation/ deflation, because that environment presents a materially positive economic environment. Likewise, falling growth was a tailwind for this asset class, which caused it to materially appreciate as equities faltered.

At the other end of the spectrum are commodities, which suffered a negative from all sides. As a rising-growth and rising-inflation-biased asset class, the fall of both factors proved to be a double whammy, which can be observed by the massive three-month drop of over 30%.

Keep in mind that these are far from precise measures. Do not attempt to calculate the exact impact from each factor to assess the expected asset-class return. The focus should be on direction and rough magnitude to demonstrate the cause-effect relationship between the economic environment (growth and inflation), and attractiveness of cash to the various asset-class returns. Again, the key is to appreciate the main influence on asset-class returns to better understand why the returns played out as they did. The repeated cause-effect connection also helps reinforce the logic supporting the risk party portfolio construction process. We allocate to the selected asset classes because they are reliably diverse. When you observe the asset classes behaving as expected during various growth and inflation environments, you can gain greater confidence in the cause-effect relationship. Then, by overlaying the impact of the attractiveness of cash, you can gain a more refined understanding of additional inputs into asset-class price changes. You will also see in real time the simultaneous impact on asset classes from these two factors. This insight should also make it less likely that you will sell during these environments, because you will better understand why the portfolio may be down and why the forward-looking returns probably will improve.

ABSOLUTE VERSUS RELATIVE UNDERPERFORMANCE

Thus far I have addressed environments during which the risk parity portfolio may perform poorly from an absolute return perspective. That is, when it is biased to underperform cash. As shown, risk parity has and should be expected to compare favorably to cash over most time periods. The calendar years during which it trailed cash are relatively few in number, and the losing periods are for the most part modest in magnitude. Moreover, in the calendar years after a downturn risk parity delivered outsized returns, averaging over 10% per annum in calendar years following a negative excess return year. In short, from an absolute return angle, risk parity has outperformed stocks over the past 50-plus years and has provided materially superior downside protection. These characteristics should be the goal of any long-term investment strategy.

In practice, however, investors have a tendency to use the stock market as a reference point to determine success or failure of an investment strategy over shorter time frames. Absolute returns go out the window when stocks are roaring. This is because the focus of the media and popular press is to talk about the performance of the "market," which is specific to the stock market (as opposed to other markets like Treasuries, TIPS, or commodities). In fact, it has become common to equate investing with simply investing in companies via stock purchases.

This bias actually makes it more challenging to successfully implement a risk parity strategy in practice. Stocks are volatile and can enjoy fabulous bull markets for extended periods (of course, they can suffer terrible bear markets as well). When the reference point is the stock market (as opposed to cash), the risk parity portfolio will obviously underperform equities when equities are the best-performing asset class. Likewise, risk parity should outperform when equities are the worst performing and fall somewhere in the middle the rest of the periods.

Table 13.3 provides the percentage of time during which the risk parity portfolio outperformed global equities since 1970. We analyze "rolling" periods starting with 1 month and extending to 20 years. This window into historical results shows us at any point in time how likely we would have been to conclude that risk parity was doing well or poorly versus the stock market.

Table 13.3 Percentage of Time Risk Parity Portfolio Beat Global Equities – January 1970 to March 2021

Rolling Period				
Month	Quarter	1 Year	5 Years	20 Years
48%	48%	50%	57%	69%

Source: Bloomberg.

The key takeaway is that the risk parity portfolio has underperformed global equities about half the time over shorter time frames (and therefore outperformed about half the time). However, over longer periods it has demonstrated greater consistency in outperforming stocks. This should not come as a surprise. The longer the measurement period, the more likely risk parity is to outperform, because we know that it beat stocks over the full 50-plus-year period with greater consistency and less risk. Over shorter periods it can underperform since stocks are more volatile and can swing around with greater dispersion versus the steadier risk parity portfolio. This also reflects the return distribution profile of stocks, which have historically exhibited negative "skew" and "fat tails." That is, stocks have historically enjoyed longer periods of positive performance and short periods of sharp declines.

This is an absolutely critical point that you should recognize up front. If the reference point is cash, then you'll be satisfied with risk parity's performance the majority of the time. If you are constantly comparing it to stocks, then you'll only be happy about half the time (even though over the full period you should come out ahead with less risk). I point this out so that you don't overreact when these environments inevitably transpire. You should actually expect this outcome!

The big risk in practice is you invest in risk parity and then when it trails equities for a long enough period during which your patience runs out, you switch to a more traditional equity-dominated allocation. The way to protect yourself from getting whipsawed in this manner is to focus on beating cash over time and expect stretches of underperformance versus equities. You can shift your focus by appreciating that over the very long run you can expect superior returns with less risk by emphasizing this new perspective.

You may also compare the risk parity portfolio to 60/40, which has comparable risk. Table 13.4 shows the percentage of time risk parity outperformed the conventional balanced mix.

Table 13.4 Percentage of Time Risk Parity Portfolio Beat 60/40 – January 1970 to March 2021

Rolling Period				
Month	Quarter	1 Year	5 Years	20 Years
51%	52%	61%	64%	73%

Source: Bloomberg.

It makes sense that the risk parity portfolio beats 60/40 more frequently than it outperforms equities since equities have a higher expected return than 60/40.

Finally, I compare risk parity to cash in Table 13.5. After all, it is cash that we are ultimately trying to outperform over time from an absolute return perspective.

Table 13.5   Percentage of Time Risk Parity Portfolio Beat Cash – January 1970 to March 2021

Rolling Period				
Month	Quarter	1 Year	5 Years	20 Years
59%	65%	73%	92%	100%

Source: Bloomberg.

The results should not surprise you at this point. The strong balance inherent in the risk parity portfolio has historically enabled it to outpace cash the vast majority of rolling periods.

SUMMARY

With the close of this chapter, we have come full circle. I presented the conceptual framework for building a balanced asset allocation. I then walked through the key factors that influence asset-class returns and described how to select asset classes that are biased to perform differently during shifting economic environments. I covered how to structure each asset class to deliver comparable returns and risk over the long run. I then described the process for determining the target allocation to each market segment to construct a well-diversified risk parity portfolio that is not overly sensitive to the performance of any single asset class or economic environment. I evaluated historical returns going back to 1970 and, in the case of Treasuries and stocks, all the way back to 1926. The benefits of a more balanced portfolio over the long run are compelling and reliable. I discussed the added boost that comes from regular rebalancing to further improve long-term returns. Efficient implementation of the strategy was covered in Chapter 12 to assist in taking the concepts presented here and putting them into practice. Finally, in this chapter, I presented the environments during which you may expect risk parity to underperform (both in absolute and relative terms) to hopefully arm you with better-informed insights to prevent selling at lows in the future. In Chapter 14, I provide answers to the most frequently asked questions that I have received from clients and prospective investors over the past 15 years.

CHAPTER FOURTEEN

FAQs

As a proponent of the risk parity approach over the past 15 years, I have had the opportunity to hear a wide range of questions and concerns about the strategy. Certain topics seem to surface more frequently. These recurring inquiries have also enabled me to formulate clear responses and refine answers that appear to resonate with investors. This chapter offers a summary of the most commonly raised questions and my respective replies.

DOES IT MAKE SENSE TO OWN LONG DURATION BONDS WITH LOW INTEREST RATES?

This is probably the most frequently asked question about and/or objection to the risk parity portfolio. The argument generally goes something along these lines, "Interest rates can only go up from today's low levels. Therefore, it seems like an obviously bad investment to buy long-dated bonds since they have low projected returns and high risk."

My response will be divided into the two core components of the typical concerns raised:

1. Low potential returns due to low starting yields
2. High potential risk due to rising yields

Concerns about Low Potential Returns

The current yield provides the exact return an investor realizes if a Treasury bond is *held to maturity*. Thus, a yield that is incontrovertibly near historic lows provides ample support for the concern about low future returns. When viewed through this lens, long-term Treasuries can understandably look unattractive.

There are a few problems with this perspective. First, the low yield of Treasuries corresponds to the even lower yield of cash. In fact, cash rates are at zero at the time of this writing and have hovered at or near zero since 2009. The rock bottom cash rate has lowered the expected return of Treasuries as it has that of *every other asset class*. Recall that each asset class provides a risk premium above cash. When cash is far below its historical average (which is about 4%), then the expected return of all asset classes will be commensurately lower. This is most obvious with Treasuries because its future return can be more precisely calculated than that of equities, commodities, and TIPS. However, the long-term impact of lower cash rates applies across the board, even for asset classes where the math is less obvious.

The second problem with overemphasizing the current low yield is that long-term Treasuries can actually produce high returns over shorter time frames. For instance, during the first quarter of 2020, when global stocks plunged about 21%, long Treasuries surged by 21% (precisely when high returns were most needed). In Chapter 4 I showed a similar pattern in prior bear markets over the past 20 years when equities fell by 20% or more. Long-term TIPS exhibited a similar outcome. The reason this happened is that in each case economic growth underperformed what was discounted and that predictably caused interest rates to fall. This occurred despite the fact that rates were already low before the surprising economic contraction. I clearly remember talk of historically low interest rates emerging in the mid-2000s when investors began to question how low rates could go. The bottom line is that the yield curve prices-in future expected cash rates, and if there is a downside economic shock that was not expected (note that none of them are), then the market will price-in the new information with lower long-term interest rates. This mechanically boosts the price of assets like long-dated Treasuries.

A good example of the potential upside of government bonds can be found in Japan. In the early 1990s, yields on Japanese government bonds were very low, yet this was one of the best-performing asset classes during the decade because rates fell even further.

Next, you may recall that the Treasury exposure that I proposed was through the use of Treasury futures as opposed to physical bonds. Treasury futures earn the excess return of long-term Treasuries over cash. As a result, the future return has more to do with the slope of the yield curve (the difference between the yield of a long-term Treasury bond and the rate of cash), than it does the starting yield. This is because the spread is what the investors earn and not the absolute yield. Therefore, if cash is yielding 6% and the long bond yields 7%, then the excess is only 1%. However, if cash is at 0% and the long bond offers 3%, then the spread in our example is actually much higher when cash is at 0%. Further, even if the yield curve is inverted (meaning that cash rates are greater than long rates), that doesn't mean "negative" expected excess returns, because the yield curve is an expression of the future expected rates of cash. In the first example, the weighted-average expected future cash rate is probably higher than the current cash rate, and in the second (with the inverted yield curve), it's probably lower.

Moreover, the idea of this exposure is to maintain a constant duration. This means that the bonds are not held to maturity and are rolled every quarter or year. As a result, there is a potential additional return that can accrue from "rolling down" the yield curve. In other words, when the yield curve is upward-sloping, then the yield should fall over time. By investing in a longer-dated point of the yield curve and holding for a period, selling, and then buying another futures contract with the original maturity, you have the opportunity to earn an additional profit from the fall in yields during your hold period as your bond progresses toward its maturity date. These two nuances of how the Treasury exposure is maintained can produce returns that may be greater than predicted by the current yield we see today.

Additionally, there is a modest amount of leverage that is applied to the Treasury (and TIPS) holdings, because they are expected to deliver returns and risk below equities and commodities, even at the longer durations of most longer-dated bonds. Recall that modest leverage allows us to equalize expected returns and risk. One of the advantages of low yields is low financing cost for utilizing leverage. That is, the low yields that concern most investors actually have some benefits due to historically low borrowing expenses.

Finally, and perhaps most important, the return of bonds need not be high to be valuable. A common oversight of any single investment within the risk parity framework is the role it plays within the total portfolio.

Most investors are trained to evaluate each investment on its own merits. Instead, the focus should be on the whole and the critical role each component plays within that context. Consider that Treasuries are probably the most reliable downside growth hedge. We've seen this play out over the past several decades as Treasuries have rallied during the weakest equity environments. By balancing the portfolio in this way, we can reduce the downside risk of the total portfolio. Additionally, as covered in the chapter on the rebalancing boost (Chapter 12), two reliably diverse assets that are volatile can generate an extra return at the portfolio level. You can think of this boost as part of the benefit of including a diverse asset like long-term Treasuries in a total portfolio context. Viewing each asset class through this lens can uncover hidden virtues of assets like Treasuries, which may appear less attractive to the untrained eye. Consider, for example, if this reliable diversifier were excluded from portfolios. The downside risk would likely increase because there are few comparable replacements that can be expected to deliver potentially high returns in that particular economic environment. The question is less whether rates – and specifically the yields of the bonds you are buying – are "low" as it is whether they are as low as they can go. As long as you believe there is room for yields to fall materially from current levels in the event of a major downturn, expected returns and diversification should not be affected. If they cannot fall enough, or if the floor is even closer, both returns and diversification will suffer, and at that point, adjustments to the portfolio may be warranted.

The Risk of Rising Interest Rates

When considering the risk of rising interest rates, the existing long-term trend should be noted. Interest rates in the United States (and in many parts of the developed world) have been on a secular downtrend since the early 1980s, suggesting that an imminent reversal may not be obvious. There have been short bouts of jumping interest rates, only to be followed by even lower rates. In fact, rates in the United States are among the highest in the developed world as of this writing, despite the extremely low level relative to history. Many long-term bonds around the globe are yielding 0% or have negative rates. There are massive deflationary forces at play including high debts, which have often resulted in depressions, technological innovation that continues to bring down the cost of many goods and services, and aging demographics. Japan has been mired in a deflationary state for nearly three decades since its economy peaked in the early 1990s. All of these powerful trends should not be quickly dismissed. That is, it is not a forgone conclusion that interest rates will shortly turn the tide and go in the other direction. Given how low rates are, they will most likely rise at some point, but the timing is absolutely critical, and that is the part that is less certain. If rates continue to fall, then long-term bonds bought with cheap leverage stand to do very well. If rates stay flat, then the bonds may still do well, because the market is discounting rising rates over time. This is effectively what has happened since 2009. Cash has stayed at or near zero since then, whereas long-term rates have continually declined as cash rates repeatedly failed to rise as much as expected. This is why long-term bonds have materially outperformed cash over the past decade even though cash rates have hovered near zero.

Clearly, there is asymmetry in the potential upside and downside of interest rates the closer they get to the zero bound, meaning there is far more room for them to rise than fall. However, we should begin with why rates are so low and what these conditions say about the current economic environment. The Fed lowers rates to stimulate the economy as needed. Over the past 40 years, each successive rate reduction has been at a lower level. This process has continued until cash rates hit 0% at the onset of the Great Financial Crisis. This coincided with historically high debt levels that may have peaked. In short, as interest rates fell for decades, more and more debt had accumulated until we reached our collective debt ceiling. Since rates bottomed, the Fed has had an eye on normalizing interest rates, without success. Early attempts to raise rates resulted in a weakening economy that forced the hand of the Fed to lower rates back to zero. Most recently, a global pandemic not only brought rates back to zero once again but caused a shift in the Fed's mindset, given the enormous deflationary forces due to widespread COVID-19-related business shutdowns. Prior to COVID-19, the Fed had focused on proactively raising interest rates in anticipation of future inflation as the key lesson learned from the inflationary 1970s and 1980s. In recognition of the persistent deflationary pressures both from a secular perspective as well as the cyclical pandemic-caused forces, the Fed marked a turning point in its focus in 2020. The Fed vowed to keep rates low and quantitatively ease for as long as necessary to create inflation. It had recognized that the enemy was no longer inflation, but deflation. The Japan outcome was not as far-fetched as once thought, and too many parallels to the deflationary 1930s had emerged. In other words, we live in very challenging times that have resulted in near zero rates, and that trend may last for a while. We simply do not know what the future holds. Given these conditions and the potential range of outcomes, the need for a well-balanced portfolio is likely greater now than at any point in our lifetimes (as more fully described in Chapter 10). Treasuries and TIPS are a valuable part of that mix despite concerns about their low potential returns and risks of rising interest rates.

One concern is that asymmetry translates to greater downside risk for Treasuries and TIPS. What many miss is that low cash rates (which is why Treasury and TIPS rates are so low) also pose higher than normal downside risk for equities. The main tool of the Fed to revive an ailing economy has been to reduce the fed funds rate, which directly impacts cash rates. When rates are pinned at zero, this powerful tool becomes blunted. The Fed is limited in its traditional ability to cut interest rates to stimulate borrowing that activates a pickup in spending. Instead, the Fed is forced to resort to extraordinary measures such as quantitative easing to adequately engineer an economic recovery. The hindered stimulative tools result in greater downside risk for economic growth, which leads to increased risk for equities given their vulnerability to falling growth environments. The same can be said for other pro-growth assets such as commodities.

Additionally, an environment of rising interest rates would pose a headwind not just for Treasuries and TIPS, but all asset classes. Again, the negatives for Treasuries are simpler to see. However, as discussed in Chapter 13, all asset classes have the same bias to falling and rising cash rates, because they all compete with the risk-free rate. Ultimately, performance depends on *why* interest rates rise. In this book I've discussed the main factors that influence asset-class prices and as detailed, the economic environment is the main input.

If rates go up because of rising inflation, then the inflation hedges (TIPS, gold, and commodity producers) would be biased to outperform. Depending on the degree of change in inflation versus what was discounted, the tailwind may be enough to offset the headwind from rising cash rates. If, on the other hand, interest rates rise because of improving growth, then the assets biased to outperform in that economic environment (stocks and commodity producers) enjoy the tailwind.

The last period of sustained interest rate increases since 1970 was from March 1971 to September 1981. The 10-year Treasury yield rose from 5.5% to 15.8%. The catalyst for the spike was rising inflation, which eventually led the Fed to increase cash rates at the end of this period to bring inflation under control. Table 14.1 lists the total returns of various asset classes, 60/40, and the risk parity portfolio during this stretch, sorted from best to worst. Note that TIPS did not exist during this time.

Table 14.1   Asset-Class Returns During Rising Interest Rates – March 1971
to September 1981

Asset Class	Average Total Annualized Return
Gold	25.7%
Commodities	11.7%
Risk Parity Portfolio	**10.0%**
Cash	7.6%
Equities	5.7%
60/40	5.4%
Core Bonds	4.2%
Long-Term Treasuries	1.9%

Source: Bloomberg.

As would be expected given the economic environment of rising inflation and falling growth, gold proved to be the best-performing asset class. TIPS, which were not created until the late 1990s, would have likely performed strongly given the favorable environment. Commodities also did well because of the magnitude of the inflation increase and as a contributor to it. Risk parity came in third during this historically challenging economic climate. Remarkably, everything else underperformed cash for over a decade! Treasuries came in dead last as anticipated, but the strong balance of the risk parity portfolio plus the rebalancing boost allowed it to significantly outperform equities and a traditional 60/40 mix.

Of course, the next time rates rise it could be for very different reasons. If rising growth is the cause, then the ranking of various asset-class returns would certainly shift. Equities and commodities would likely take the lead while the falling-growth-biased assets would probably fall behind. You may notice that Treasuries do poorly in both the rising-inflation and rising-growth scenarios. This may lead you to again ask why own Treasuries since they lose in both cases? Remember that Treasuries aren't there for the rising rate environment. Instead, they protect the portfolio in periods of falling rates, which are normally associated with weakening growth (and moderate or falling inflation). Moreover, rates may stay low for an extended time, which could also benefit Treasury holders that can roll down the yield curve and lever with low financing costs. Also, we don't know the path of rates even if they were to rise. For instance, during the historic secular increase in rates during the 1970s, there were many interim periods during which rates materially declined. We've observed a similar pattern during the secular decline in rates since the early 1980s. These shifts in rates have generally corresponded with changes in the economic environment, which has consequently resulted in rallies in Treasuries over shorter time frames.

The key is to appreciate that you can own all these assets and not have to guess which way rates or inflation or growth will go next. That is the whole point of being balanced all the time. Accurately predicting the direction and timing of these major forces is very difficult. Indeed, there are many professional investors who have tried and failed. If the portfolio is well-diversified and risk balanced across all these assets, then the eventual winners and losers would offset to result in a steadier overall portfolio return, which can be seen with the attractive risk parity portfolio performance the last time interest rates rose.

One final point about rising rates is warranted. Let's say rates rise and Treasuries and possibly TIPS underperform for a period. After the rise, these assets would yield more and become more attractive looking forward. The risk parity portfolio would rebalance into these assets after their yields increase and their prices fall as part of its normal buy-low, sell-high process. Depending on how the other asset classes did, the risk parity portfolio may have held up fine and would then be in an even better position prospectively. You wouldn't have had to time when rates were going to rise because you were balanced when they did, and you rebalanced into higher-yielding bonds after the rate jump. In short, the argument is that it may be prudent to just stay balanced all the time and not worry about the timing because if you get the timing wrong, the downside risks may be enormous. Imagine if you were convinced rates were going to rise so you eliminated the Treasury holding. If you did that at the beginning of 2020, you would have lost much more during the COVID-19 downturn.

HOW DOES RISK PARITY FIT WITHIN THE TOTAL PORTFOLIO?

Typically, portfolios are subdivided into three broad categories: (1) equities, (2) fixed income, and (3) alternative investments. The last group is often a catch-all that includes everything that doesn't cleanly fit into the equity or fixed-income group. Within this framework, risk parity would fall into the alternative investments bucket for most investors since this multi-asset approach is clearly not all equities or all fixed income, even though it invests in both of those asset classes. Furthermore, it may potentially be a great complement to other alternative investments because of several unique characteristics.

Highly Liquid

First, risk parity is a liquid strategy, particularly if it is owned in a passively managed vehicle structured for liquidity like an ETF or mutual fund.

Many alternatives are less liquid or completely illiquid. I've noticed growing demand for more liquid alternative investments as the overall allocation to alternatives has generally increased over the past decade. Investors may have some liquidity considerations, so an option that is highly liquid can be attractive.

Low Fees

Risk parity should also come with low fees relative to other alternative investments, which are commonly among the most expensive investment vehicles. Because it is a less complex strategy that can effectively be passively managed, as has been described in this book, any fees charged to implement the strategy should pale in comparison to those of actively managed, multifaceted investment strategies that may require large organizations and deep research teams to successfully manage them. Risk parity, in contrast, can be easily implemented using index funds according to the concepts presented here.

Available to All Investors

Many alternative investments are only available to investors who are "qualified purchasers," which requires them to have investable assets of $5 million or more. This is a regulatory rule that exists to protect the average investor from going into complicated, nontransparent funds that they may not fully understand. The idea is that if you are ultrawealthy, then you should be financially sophisticated enough to know what you are doing. Risk parity strategies, particularly those that use an ETF or mutual fund structure, are highly regulated, relatively transparent, and publicly traded on an exchange. They are available to the entire universe of investors regardless of wealth. A risk parity hedge fund may have a $1 million minimum or higher, but a mutual fund and ETF would have extremely low minimums that any investor could afford. Also, ETFs and mutual funds are subject to the regulatory oversight of the Securities and Exchange Commission (SEC) and fall under the strict purview of the Investment Company Act of 1940. The onerous procedures mandated by these regulations are in place to protect investors from misleading investment company practices and are designed to ensure proper disclosure.

Passive versus Active

Nearly all alternative investments are actively managed strategies. Hedge funds, for instance, can go long and short in an attempt to profit from good investments as well as companies that they believe are overpriced. Mutual funds that employ alternative schemes are also typically actively managed. These funds employ various active approaches to outperform markets, such as tactically allocating across multiple asset classes or uncovering undervalued investments within market segments.

Risk parity can be either actively or passively managed. The approach described here and the one I prefer is passive, meaning that the target allocation and a rebalancing methodology are established up front, and only limited, if any, modifications are made over time. There are some actively managed risk parity funds as well that seek to outperform a passive mix over time. These approaches may try to overweight asset classes they deem to be more attractive at a point in time and underweight those that appear expensive. These shifts would be relative to whatever their neutral mix would be. Tactical changes often include increasing and decreasing total leverage based on market conditions and intent to maintain a targeted level of total portfolio volatility. One potential issue with actively managed risk parity strategies that target a certain volatility is that they are susceptible to getting whipsawed. The funds that try to control volatility do so by increasing leverage during stretches of lower market volatility and reducing leverage when market volatility is greater than normal. The idea is to have a targeted level of total portfolio volatility, say 10%, which the fund seeks to maintain. The risk with this approach is that there are countless times when low market volatility is followed by spikes in volatility and vice versa. This is exactly what happened in the first quarter of 2020. Heading into the year, market volatility was low, so a risk parity fund that targets a set volatility would have held above average leverage. Once COVID-19 hit and market volatility jumped (across asset classes), the risk parity fund that was overlevered would have experienced greater losses than it would have had if it had employed less leverage. Once the market volatility was elevated, then the risk parity fund would reduce its leverage below its long-term target to bring down the volatility of the total fund. As a result, the fund could end up underperforming during the rebound. In sum, during a V-shaped recovery, a volatility-targeting risk parity strategy could do worse on the way down and trail on the way up, compounding the underperformance over the full cycle. Conversely, a more passive approach that does not shift the portfolio leverage would not suffer the same problem. Having seen other risk parity strategies go through a similar negative experience during the 2008–2009 Global Financial Crisis, I opt for a more passive approach. A passive risk parity allocation offers the additional benefits of predictability, because there would be no reliance on the timing abilities of the fund manager, who may or may not perform as expected. Furthermore, a passive strategy should come with lower fees and greater tax efficiency due to the minimization of trading activity.

Diversification

The risk parity portfolio presented here would likely improve the diversification of the total portfolio when added. The assets in which risk parity invests are unlikely to be heavily owned by other alternative investment funds. As a result, a well-constructed risk parity strategy should offer a return stream that is different from other alternatives as well as the equity and fixed income components of the total portfolio. Indeed, one of the reasons risk parity works so well within a total portfolio is because it allocates to various asset classes that are typically underowned and structures them in a way that is less frequently used.

Transparency

One of the common drawbacks of alternative investments is that they often do not offer full transparency into the underlying holdings. Sometimes these "black-box" strategies intentionally mask their positions for fear that others will mimic their approach and effectively steal their trade secrets. After all, they charge high fees to produce attractive returns. There is real business risk in competitors trying to replicate their strategy and undercut the manager by offering it at lower fees.

Risk parity, on the other hand, should be fully transparent. This is especially true of passive approaches where the allocation is described up front and a rebalancing frequency is set. In fact, certain registered fund products (such as ETFs) typically disclose every single holding and the dollars invested in each every day on a public website. This is the opposite extreme versus most alternative investments, which are understandably far more guarded about their specific investments.

The benefit of greater transparency is a clearer understanding of the performance of the strategy relative to the market environment. For instance, if risk parity is doing poorly, it would be relatively straightforward to deduce why. You can compare publicly available index returns for equities, Treasuries, TIPS, and commodities and quickly uncover the source of the underperformance, whereas a more complex strategy may be far more challenging to decipher. This is important, because the more you understand why something is performing as it is, the more likely you are to hold on through the period of poor results, which are inevitable for any high-returning strategy. As described throughout this book, holding on can be the key to long-term success. This is particularly true when you're investing in index strategies that are more likely to revert to the mean after a stretch of underperformance as opposed to a trading strategy where the manager may have lost their edge.

Tax Efficiency

Alternative investments are notorious for being tax inefficient and compli-cated from a tax-reporting standpoint. Alternatives tend to actively trade and use esoteric securities to gain market exposures. A large number of buys and sells combined with instruments that throw off income result in relatively high taxes for many alternative strategies. In fact, these funds have the propensity to be managed for pretax-return maximization even at the expense of after-tax returns. Some of the largest investors in these funds may be institutions that don't pay taxes. Risk parity, in contrast, can and should be managed to be extremely tax efficient.

Many alternatives issue an annual K-1. Often times these tax reports are delayed and are not sent out until after the regular tax deadline of April 15, requiring tax filers to extend filing their tax returns. Mutual funds and ETFs only issue an annual 1099, similar to a basic stock or bond holding. There is typically no delay in reporting, and the taxable distributions are far easier to comprehend than a K-1.

Risk Parity as the Total Portfolio

Up to this point I have described the complementary aspects of using the risk parity portfolio as part of the alternative investment allocation *within* a total portfolio framework. There is an alternate way to think about it if you decide to fully embrace the concepts. For investors who only wish to allocate to a simple public market portfolio that excludes private assets, hedge funds, and other strategies, the risk parity portfolio could represent the entire portfolio. It is a well-diversified mix of publicly traded asset classes that is designed to deliver comparable returns to equities over the long run (if not better) with stronger downside protection and less volatil-ity. You can think of it as a more efficient approach than a 60/40 alloca-tion, which is commonly used to represent the total portfolio.

From a practical standpoint, there are two potential challenges with implementing risk parity as a total portfolio solution. First, you need complete buy in. As previously mentioned, risk parity may trail more conventional equity-dominated portfolios for extended periods (because they are less balanced). The odds of switching out after underperformance increase, unless there is unwavering confidence in the approach. Second, an efficient way to implement risk parity may be to do it through a mutual fund or ETF, as an individual might invest in a typical asset allocation or target-date fund in a 401(k). The potential issue with that is if it makes up the entire portfolio, a single line item, despite being more diversified than a 60/40 allocation, may feel overly concentrated. Of course, to combat this concern you may implement the exact same strategy on a separate account basis (assuming you can live with the line-item risk previously described), or simply look through to the fund holdings on a regular basis.

DO ASSET CLASS GAINS AND LOSSES NET OUT TO ZERO?

A common question that has surfaced over the years is related to the notion that the asset classes within the risk parity are supposed to go up and down in different environments. An incorrect conclusion many reach is that the gains and losses of the varying markets net out to zero. In other words, something goes up and another thing goes down about the same amount, so the end result is no gain.

This is an inaccurate assumption. As a reminder, the risk parity portfolio invests across a diverse set of asset classes, each of which has a *positive expected return* over time. The way to think about the variations over time is that each asset class is biased to outperform and underperform *its average return* during particular growth and inflation environments. For instance, equities may average 5% excess returns above cash over the long run. During favorable periods, equities may deliver 10% above cash (or 5% above average) and when a bad environment transpires, equities may be flat versus cash (or 5% below average). If the main reason for the variation is inflation, then commodities may produce the opposite return pattern by beating their average by 5% when equities underperform their average and vice versa. The net result is the investor earns the average excess return of the asset classes (5% above cash in this example) as opposed to zero.

Said differently and perhaps even more simply, if each asset class has an expected return that is above zero, then combining them can't result in a zero return. This is not to say that there won't be shorter periods during which the net result may be zero or negative. A quick glimpse of historical returns certainly demonstrates this point. However, over the long run, the total return of the risk parity portfolio is anticipated to be relatively attractive versus cash and on an absolute basis. You may refer back to Chapter 9 on historical returns for long-term results as support.

DOES DIVERSIFICATION WORK DURING A CRISIS?

A commonly held misperception about diversification is that during a crisis, all correlations go to one, resulting in all assets contemporaneously losing money. That is, diversification fails to protect investors when it is most needed. I feel that this myth exists because most investors are not sufficiently diversified. They typically don't hold the most diversifying assets such as those within the risk parity allocation. For instance, during material economic downturns when equities generally take a massive hit, long-term Treasuries, long-term TIPS, and gold have historically performed strongly. Conversely, some of the more commonly used diversifiers like high-yield bonds and hedge funds have demonstrated stronger correlations during periods of crisis. Table 14.2 compares returns of these asset classes during the last four major crisis periods when equities dropped by at least 20% from peak to trough.

Table 14.2   Various Asset-Class Cumulative Returns During Last Four Bear Markets

Asset Class	2020 COVID-19 Pandemic (Jan 2020– Mar 2020)	2011 Eurozone Crisis (May 2011– Sep 2011)	2008 Credit Crisis (Nov 2007– Feb 2009)	2000 Dot-Com Crash (Apr 2000– Sep 2002)
Global Equities	−21%	−20%	−54%	−47%
Long-Term Treasuries	**+21%**	**+26%**	**+17%**	**+35%**
Long-Term TIPS	**+9%**	**+15%**	**−2%**	**+45%**
Gold	**+4%**	**+4%**	**+18%**	**+16%**
High-Yield Bonds	−13%	−7%	−26%	−8%
Hedge Funds	−12%	−9%	−21%	−2%

Source: Bloomberg.

Note that the returns of high-yield bonds and the broad hedge fund index were highly correlated to the downside during major equity drawdowns. Meanwhile, Treasuries, TIPS, and gold served as powerful diversifiers just when equities suffered a major bear market. Equities plunged an average of 35% from peak to trough over these four periods of crisis, while the three diversifiers delivered an average return of 17% to the upside. As evidenced by solid returns during these bear markets, the correlation during the crisis actually came in closer to *negative one!*

That is not to say that there weren't brief times within these bear markets when Treasuries, TIPS, and/or gold may have declined in value. In Chapter 13 I explained the rare and short-lived environments during which all assets may simultaneously fall. But as can be seen, over the full peak-to-trough fall of equities, these diversifiers performed as would be expected.

The most interesting aspect of these diversifiers is that they also offer an attractive long-term return. This is in contrast to most hedges or insurance policies that come with a cost for portfolio protection. For instance, you can limit the downside of your stock portfolio by purchasing put options. However, this insurance has a negative long-term expected return since you have to pay a premium for the protection. Fire or auto insurance works the same way; you pay a premium to the insurance company and lose money every year that you don't make a claim (which is the vast majority of years). In aggregate, the insurance companies make a profit because they collect more in premiums than they pay in claims even if some clients come out ahead.

As shown in Chapter 9 on long-term historical returns of the asset classes in the risk parity portfolio, all have achieved attractive positive returns. As a result, you are able to secure many of the benefits that come with portfolio insurance without the negative cost.

IF RISK PARITY IS SO OBVIOUS, WHY ISN'T EVERYONE INVESTING THIS WAY?

I asked Ray Dalio the exact same question many years ago and found his response enlightening. There tends to be a widespread follow-the-herd mentality in society. This bias is particularly apparent in the investment industry. We go to school and are taught the fundamentals of various subjects. Those who are able to absorb and regurgitate the information on an exam earn high grades. Strong marks open doors to better schools that repeat the process until we graduate into the real world. When we begin employment, we are again trained in the preexisting processes established at our workplace. Those who listen well rise through the ranks, and they become the trainers for the next generation.

Although we are sometimes encouraged to think independently, the vast majority of people simply focus on learning the rules of the game. Some are better at playing than others, which essentially separates the winners from the losers. Every now and then, an extraordinary talent comes along who bucks the trend and has the perspective to see what others don't. Sufficient success may spawn a new trend that others follow, and the cycle repeats.

In short, the current system isn't exactly set up to foster extensive independent thinking. Instead, inertia tends to result in the way things are being done to stay that way until it has become apparent to the majority that it no longer works well. These cycles can take a long time to play out. The existence of peer risk can further prolong the status quo as well.

For these reasons, the risk parity concepts may not become mainstream for some time even if the framework is sounder than the traditional approach. It can simply take an extended period of time to convert the conventional mix to something that may make more sense. It may even require a prolonged stretch of outperformance for the newer methods to overtake the old guard.

The other aspect that may partially explain the gap between the current traditional mix and risk parity is the latter requires a completely different mindset. The rationale for a 60/40 allocation is fairly straightforward: stocks are risky and high returning so including safer bonds helps bring down the total portfolio risk to an acceptable level. Risk parity, on the other hand, focuses on diversifying across multiple asset classes biased to perform differently in varying economic environments. It then takes the step of structuring each asset class to deliver comparable returns and risk. Clearly, this is a more involved and thoughtful approach to building a well-balanced asset allocation than the traditional 60/40 construct. For this reason, thus far it has been most broadly accepted by sophisticated institutional investors and limited high net worth individuals. In fact, there have not been many books written on risk parity to date. Indeed, one of the goals of this book is to describe the process in simple-to-understand terms and concepts to appeal to a wide audience of interested investors. Ultimately, the objective is to spark more interest in the framework and develop a greater following for a more efficient portfolio strategy than current convention.

DOES REBALANCING MORE OR LESS FREQUENTLY MAKE A BIG DIFFERENCE?

We have analyzed different rebalancing methodologies and have found that the biggest improvement comes from doing rebalancing versus not rebalancing at all. Our research shows minimal difference between various frequencies of rebalancing. Table 14.3 compares the returns of the risk parity portfolio with no rebalancing, annual rebalancing, quarterly rebalancing, and monthly rebalancing. I compare results over two different time frames – since January 1970 and since April 1998 – to cover the full risk parity portfolio with TIPS and the longer history with the TIPS substitute.

Table 14.3 Risk Parity Portfolio Results with Various Rebalancing Frequencies

Asset Class	No Rebalancing	Annual Rebalancing	Quarterly Rebalancing	Monthly Rebalancing
Risk Parity Portfolio January 1970 to March 2021	10.3%	10.9%	10.8%	10.7%
Risk Parity Portfolio April 1998 to March 2021	8.0%	9.4%	9.6%	9.2%

Source: Bloomberg and Evoke Advisors analysis.

The main argument for more frequent rebalancing is that it helps the portfolio stay closer to the target allocation to ensure proper balance all the time. The other side of the argument is it may be better to let the various asset classes run a little bit in order to earn a greater return boost from momentum as the winners gain more and the losers get cheaper. In reality, the data clearly demonstrates little disparity between monthly, quarterly, or annual rebalancing. This is probably because the two aforementioned benefits (staying balanced more often versus greater rebalancing boost) effectively offset one another. There is some randomness with the data set so there's no sense in reading too much into the results posted in Table 14.3. The main takeaway is that doing some rebalancing is definitely better than not rebalancing. You may also notice that the rebalancing boost has been greater when there are more diversifying assets in the portfolio as evidenced by the bigger difference between no rebalancing and some rebalancing for the risk parity portfolio since 1970 versus since 1998 (which involves a more diversified portfolio). This result is logical since there is greater opportunity to buy low and sell high when the number of diverse assets is greater.

The other consideration in practice is that more frequent rebalancing may incur additional transaction costs and/or be less tax efficient. Thus, additional inputs should be factored in when determining the best rebalancing program for your portfolio. Within certain managed vehicle structures, the tax impact from rebalancing can by and large be ignored.

CHAPTER FIFTEEN

Conclusion

Since I launched my investment career in 1999, I have endeavored to learn as much as I could from others. In the beginning I was astounded by nearly everyone I met. Over time, I started to realize that most investment professionals think alike and believe in the same core investment tenets. Given the competitive landscape, I gradually developed a tendency to be most attracted to special investors who I sensed possessed unique insight. Over the past couple of decades, I have had the good fortune to be surrounded by, and engaged in, deep conversations with some of the sharpest minds in the investment world. Being entrusted to manage billions of dollars by sophisticated investors can open doors that would otherwise be inaccessible, providing fertile ground for absorbing as much insight as desired.

This book provides a synthesis of an investment philosophy that makes more sense to me than any other I've heard over the years. I don't prefer risk parity just because it is different, but because the conceptual framework is logically sound and is supported by compelling long-term data that I've personally analyzed. I've used this framework to invest billions of dollars over the past 15 years and have firsthand experience with all its pros and cons.

My goal here has been to introduce you to this unique way of building a balanced asset allocation so you can independently decide for yourself what makes the most sense. My aim was to present the argument objectively in a format that was readable and understandable by those interested in investing. As I have stressed throughout this book, I also feel that an educated investor is more likely to make good decisions while implementing an investment strategy in practice. I've seen far too many investors repeatedly buy high and sell low. I believe a deeper appreciation of the full picture of the risk parity philosophy will assist investors in gaining sufficient knowledge to hold on through inevitable stretches of relative underperformance so they can enjoy its long-term benefits. Ultimately, that is the hardest part about investing. It's easy to hold on to whatever is working well. The real test comes when the strategy is temporarily out of favor. My hope is you now have the understanding and conviction to stay the course. I wish you long-term investment success.

Index